T0194667

BETWEEN CULTURES

PHRONESIS

Since 1989, when the first book was published in the Phronesis series, many events have taken place which initially brought the hope that great possibilities were opening up for the extension and deepening of democracy. Disenchantment, however, came quickly and what we witnessed instead was the reinforcement and generalization of the neoliberal hegemony. Today, the left-wing project is in an even deeper crisis than ten years ago. An increasing number of social-democratic parties, under the pretence of 'modernizing' themselves, are discarding their left identity. According to the advocates of the 'third way', with the advent of globalization the time has come to abandon the old dogmas of Left and Right and promote a new entrepreneurial spirit at all levels of society.

Phronesis's objective is to establish a dialogue among all those who assert the need to redefine the Left/Right distinction – which constitutes the crucial dynamic of modern democracy – instead of relinquishing it. Our original concern, which was to bring together left-wing politics and the theoretical developments around the critique of essentialism, is more pertinent than ever. Indeed, we still believe that the most important trends in contemporary theory – deconstruction, psychoanalysis, the philosophy of language as initiated by the later Wittgenstein and post-Heideggerian hermeneutics – are the necessary conditions for understanding the widening of social struggles characteristic of the present stage of democratic politics, and for formulating a new vision for the Left in terms of radical and plural democracy.

BETWEEN CULTURES

Tensions in the struggle for recognition

$\blacklozenge$

ALEXANDER GARCÍA DÜTTMANN

Translated by Kenneth B. Woodgate

VERSO

London • New York

First published by Verso 2000
© Alexander García Düttmann 2000
All rights reserved

The moral rights of the author and translator have been asserted

Verso
UK: 6 Meard Street, London W1V 3HR
USA: 180 Varick Street, New York, NY 10014–4606

Verso is the imprint of New Left Books

ISBN 1–85984–755–2
ISBN 1–85984–273–9 (pbk)

British Library Cataloguing in Publication Data
A catalogue record for this book is available from the British Library

Library of Congress Cataloging-in-Publication Data
A catalog record for this book is available from the Library of Congress

Typeset by The Running Head Limited, www.therunninghead.com
Printed by Biddles Ltd, Guildford and King's Lynn

For Hugo Santiago

'Who whom?'

Bertolt Brecht, *Mr Puntila and His Man Matti*

CONTENTS

CONTENTS

TRANSLATOR'S NOTE

In English the word *recognition* is used to render a number of German terms. These terms have been translated as accurately and consistently as possible, but a reading of this book will be more rewarding if the following distinctions are kept in mind from the outset:

recognition, recognizing (*Anerkennung, anerkennen*) is used in the sense of acknowledgement;

re-cognition, re-cognizing (*Erkenntnis, erkennen*) is used in a cognitive sense, and refers to the identification of something as such;

repeated re-cognition (*Wiedererkennen*) refers to the identifying act through which one finds oneself in the other, or through which one finds something in what it is not, thereby overcoming otherness.

With regard to foreign-language sources, the original text is taken to be the authoritative version. Published English translations of quoted sources have been used wherever possible, but at times it has been necessary to modify these when nuances of the original text's meaning have been lost. Where only foreign-language sources exist, the English versions are my own translations. These have been checked with the author to ensure consistency between the source's meaning and the text's argument.

K.B.W.

DIAGNOSIS AND THOUGHT

In a time of general restoration, which inevitably conceals the precariousness, invalidity or unacceptability of that which is restored, one single slogan holds: *risk rebellion and revolt.* Restoration claims the concept of recognition to ensure political, social and intellectual integration; at the same time it reproduces the repression and conformity which supposedly are to be overcome through the recognition of the other. One must therefore wrest the concept of recognition from restoration, one must reinvent it and use it against restoration's apologists, in cultures, between cultures. The opposition of disintegration and integration serves the integrated as justification for and means of intimidation; in truth this opposition merely prolongs their impotence when faced with the reaction of the disintegrated. One must dismantle this opposition at that point where the integrated and the disintegrated play out their restorational intentions, plans and actions against each other. One must look for those tensions in the struggle for recognition which are brought about by a crack, by incommensurable approaches, not by integratable demands that can be raised with a clear conscience, not by ideologies whose radical appearance merely provides an excuse for the restoration of political or religious fundamentalism. In the incommensurability of approaches with which rebellion and revolt begin, in the *re-fusal* to recognize and in the *revocation* which does not aim for the recognition of another restoration, lies the opportunity to touch the limits of (affirmative) recognition and to uncover the possibility of a change that no longer bears the features of restoration.

BETWEEN CULTURES

Cultural trash

Someone wants to be recognized as this or that because he or she claims to be this or that. In other words, someone wants to be recognized on the grounds of having accomplished this or that, of belonging to this or that group, to this or that culture, to this or that tradition, to this or that linguistic community. For it is not the pure fact of being, not the contingent isolation of an individual existence that justifies the demand for recognition, but rather the cultural mediation of a belonging, the cultural testimony which consists in having achieved a result.

Recognition must consequently establish *and* confirm an identity. By constituting *and* authenticating an identity, recognition is meant to incorporate a contingent *I* into the community of a deeply rooted We, a We firmly anchored and clearly positioned. The one who recognizes is both a witness *and* a producer. He belongs to a presupposed community or society which must first be formed by recognition. But recognition never forms such a society or community, given that the very moment it tries to unite what it produces and what it witnesses, what it produces in what it witnesses and what it witnesses in what it produces, it must indicate its own splitting into reception and spontaneity, confirmation and establishment, witnessing and producing. There is no community or society formed by recognition which does not also fall apart and which is not always open to a different recognition, to the revocation or possible absence of recognition. The voice with which recognition endows or seeks to endow the one who is to be recognized, is neither the echo of a heard voice, of a voice to which recognition testifies, nor is it the unheard sound of a voice produced by recognition. Through recognition, a voice one does not have is lost and a voice one already has is won. In principle, the one who recognizes and the one who is recognized do not know which voice is which. Otherwise nothing would be lost and nothing would be won. The confirmation would be a production, the production a confirmation. The testimony, the evidence of the witness would reside in the production of the witnessed. What else would this be but the idealism of an absolute recognition which denies or endures its heterogeneity?

Recognition is, in short, the impossible creation of what is given. Its double heterogeneous function and its double heterogeneous effect, its performative and its constative aspect, its destabilizing double character as act and statement, the simultaneity of irreconcilable features, create a tension within recognition, the tension of a being-not-one. Recognition is not-one because it cannot be identified and determined as this or that act. It cannot be simply and fully re-cognized. Perhaps recognition itself needs to be recognized. Its performative aspect, the creative, inventive, productive side of recognition, the instituting or establishing act without which there is no identity, affects the very presupposition of this identity. Recognition does not leave the presupposed identity of the one who is to be recognized untouched. If act and statement, establishment and confirmation were to coincide without remainder, then the establishment would be a mere confirmation and not really an establishment, or the confirmation would ultimately prove to be nothing but an establishment. As a performative act aimed at establishing, producing, constituting an identity, recognition may and must indeed be ruled by conventions. It is already guided by the constative moment of recognition, by its confirming and stating moment. However, the openness of an unforeseeable future throws the act of recognition off balance; as a consequence, the transition from the contingent to the necessary, from the incidental to the justified and stable cannot completely succeed. To the extent that what is established is never simply something which has been confirmed, to the extent that the act of establishment displaces what is being presupposed, not allowing it to maintain its position, that which is recognized or that which is to be recognized appears itself to be not-one. That which is to be recognized is not itself; it is neither a contingent and isolated I, nor does it belong to a stable We. Yet only if it is not itself, only if it is not-one, only if it is at odds with itself, can it claim recognition.

Perhaps it is possible to formulate some kind of axiom on the basis of these introductory remarks. *Aiming for identity, recognition brings about non-identity and is brought about by non-identity.* For the non-identical wants to be heard, it 'seeks to be audible', it looks for an expression, an utterance or a voice, as Adorno puts it. The question of recognition is thus the question of a voice which cannot be assigned to the identity of a speaker and which cannot be discerned in its identity or unity by a cognitive or re-cognizing act. It is the question of the voice of the non-identical.

Why can one not recognize that which is only itself, that which is nothing but a natural given, that which remains in its very being or becoming? It seems plausible to assume that for there to be recognition, some claim, some demand, some request must come into play. This explains why reasons must be sought

5

and provided for recognition. Recognition responds to a demand or to a claim and hence is not an unjustified act, an act without a ground on which to rest. That which can be recognized is something which ought to be recognized, something which seeks to justify its claim to validity. It implicitly or explicitly raises a claim which it must substantiate; it must prove that the claim it raises is a justified claim. If recognition is something claimed or demanded, then that which is to be recognized never simply remains in its being or becoming as a self-same entity, an entity identical to itself. That which demands recognition differs from itself. It comes out, as it were, it goes beyond itself, distances itself from itself without being able to return to itself in a self-referential turn. The fact that it demands recognition means that it is not yet what it is, that it must first show itself to be this or that and thereby assert itself.

However, a recognition which does justice to a demand, allowing what is to be recognized to be this or that and to assert itself, cannot be a completely justified act, an act rendered entirely intelligible. A demand is not defined by the justifiability of what it demands. The justifiability of what it demands determines only whether a demand may be regarded as legitimate or not. It determines whether a claim to validity can be fulfilled and generalized, or whether one must reject it on the grounds of its being inadmissible. Claims and demands are made wherever one cannot exclude the possibility that what is claimed and demanded proves to be unjustified or unjustifiable and is rejected, indeed that it is rejected without its justifiability having been checked. It is for this reason that demands and claims are more than simply justified or unjustified, at least at the time they are made. The element or the medium they require for their development is the openness of an irreducible uncertainty which, if it is to be an uncertainty, must not be interpreted as a potential certainty.

Uncertainty is the medium, the element of claims and demands, but it also traverses or permeates them. A claim must be recognized as a claim, a demand demands recognition as a demand; therefore they both expose themselves to the uncertainty of a recognition which splits into a confirmation and an establishment. For a demand raised in the midst of an uncertainty tests itself as a demand. Its being-raised is no self-assertion. Whenever a demand for recognition is raised explicitly, it has already demanded recognition.

As element and medium in which a demand and a claim are raised, uncertainty bestows an unconditional aspect upon them. To this unconditionality one must react with an unconditional response which must be suspended, too. Only if something in the demand points beyond the possibility of its justification, a possibility which comprises its determination as an unjustified demand, only if an unconditional response is thereby provoked, can one rightly speak of a demand or a claim to validity, irrespective of the differences which distinguish the usage of the word 'claim' and the word 'demand' in ordinary language; a demand seems to address the other more directly, while claims seem to be closely linked to the conviction of an entitlement. Demands and claims to validity raise the question of why something is being demanded and claimed; they raise the question of the justifiability and the specific meaning of that which is being claimed and demanded. However, by raising this question they also create a tension between two irreconcilable responses, between the unconditionality of an *acte gratuit* and the conditionality of a discursive fulfilment *determined* by arguments and justified by the recourse to reasons. The one who recognizes and the one who is to be recognized are murderers and poets; they are reminiscent of the sniper in Buñuel's *Phantom of Liberty*, who without motivation and without discriminating his targets shoots

7

into the crowd from the upper floors of the Tour Montparnasse. Because demands and claims exceed their justifiability, because their justifiability entails a necessary uncertainty, they are both characterized by an unconditional aspect, by something violent, blind and unacceptable from the point of view of philosophy.

The recognition which asks for reasons and which is itself asked to provide reasons, never amounts to more than a more or less justified act, precisely because it reacts to a demand, to a claim for validity. It only partially suits aims of social integration, of incorporation or inclusion into the community of a We.

Nevertheless, the uncertainty of the demand also involves the possibility that the response fails to emerge. Stanley Cavell points to this possibility in an essay which discusses the meaning and the relevance of the experience of pain and suffering. He distinguishes recognition or acknowledgement from knowledge. On the one hand, knowledge and acknowledgement are essentially different from each other, as one can tell when comparing a mere absence of knowledge to a failure to acknowledge. The failure to acknowledge and to meet the demand for recognition, the absence of a recognizing response is not just an absence, as in the case of a missing knowledge. It gives proof of something, for example an aberration, a certain indifference or coldness. The absent recognition is an omission. Cavell does not, however, take into account the possibility that the demand for recognition, the demand for something to be acknowledged, remains unanswered because there is no one, or because it finds no one, who could hear it: 'The point is that the concept of acknowledgment is evidenced equally by its failure as by its success' (Cavell, 263).

On the other hand, knowledge is not simply different from acknowledgement; as knowledge it also requires acknowledgement or recognition. One cannot know at all what it means for the other to experience pain, if the demand for recognition derived from the expressed experience is not fulfilled. The mere knowledge, the pure certainty that the other experiences pain is not enough to grasp the significance and the meaning of this feeling, or indeed to grasp what this feeling is. Here, grasping is not to be understood as a cognitive comprehension, as a mirroring confirmation, as a re-cognition, but depends on the activity, on the action, on the act of acknowledging or recognizing:

> It is not enough that I *know* (am certain) that you suffer – I must do or reveal something (whatever can be done). In a word, I must *acknowledge* it, otherwise I do not know what '(your or his) being in pain' means. Is. (ibid.)

Are the failure to meet the demand for recognition and the absence of a recognizing response relevant, significant, meaningful for the knowledge and the re-cognition which provide certainty? If knowledge is reliant on acknowledgement and recognition in order to constitute itself as knowledge, in order to be a knowledge of what the pain of the other is, then the failing recognition or the absence of a response may suggest an absence of knowledge – an absence which does not *determine* the failure of recognition, given that it is inseparable from it: 'If one says that this is a *failure* to acknowledge another's suffering, surely this would not mean that we fail, in such cases, to *know* that he is suffering? It may or it may not' (ibid.).

How can the omission of a recognition indicate an absence of knowledge and yet not do so? Surely for the following reason. Knowledge cannot constitute itself as knowledge without fulfilling a demand for recognition, at least in the case of the other's experience of pain; however, recognition can never fail in such a way that it no longer points to itself as a failing recognition – knowledge cannot be simply absent, not if it is to depend on recognition in its very constitution. Consequently one must ask whether Cavell does not restrict the pertinence of the distinction he introduces, the pertinence of the distinction between an absence of knowledge and the omission of a recognition, between a description and an evaluation, between a certainty and an acknowledgement. Recognition, it seems, must always be understood as the *need for knowledge* and as the *neediness of knowledge*.

Yet what effect does the uncertainty of the demand for recognition, an uncertainty implied in the possibility that a response fails to emerge or that the fulfilment of the demand does not occur, have on the demand itself? Must one not go so far as to question the possibility of an entirely successful recognition? Is not every successful recognition overshadowed by the fact that it might have failed? Does not the possibility of an absence which must not necessarily be an omission (a response can fail to emerge because there is no one to hear the demand) cast its shadow on every successful recognition? Must one not conclude from the impossibility of an entirely successful recognition, that the demand for recognition can never be raised as a simple demand, a demand entirely successful as a demand? Is the demand for recognition not itself affected by the uncertainty without which it could not be raised, by the uncertainty which is given with the possibility of an omission or an absence?

One can say that a demand is marked by an uncertainty because every demand requires uncertainty as the medium in which it is raised. One can say that a demand is marked by an uncertainty because nothing ensures that a response will ensue, whether the one who makes the demand encounters indifference or whether there is no one to hear the demand. Finally one can say that a demand is marked by an uncertainty because the seriousness of a demand (for recognition) cannot be guaranteed; on each occasion one must decide anew whether another person's demand (for recognition) is feigned or whether it is meant seriously. Even if one decides beforehand that the principle of charity, a regulating mechanism which does not distinguish and discriminate against those who make a demand, is to be applied to any interaction with others, seriousness is by no means immune to irony and intrigue.

Recognition, something one more or less demands and justifies, something one demands and justifies more or less seriously, is unthinkable in mere nature. It is unthinkable in both first and second nature, for it is just as alien to a state of second nature where everything has received its proper determination, as it is to a state of first nature where a being is nothing but precisely this or that being. Recognition becomes an issue when nature opens itself up and turns into something else, into culture. However, recognition can be an issue only as long as culture does not close itself off, turning into second nature. If recognition has no definable place because it constantly occurs *in between*, if this is what we mean when we say that it is related to a claim or a demand, then it must be assumed that only that which to a certain extent remains opaque, only that which resists comprehension or cognitive determination, only that which can forget itself, may indeed be recognized. There is no recognition without *self-forgetfulness*. That which is recognized and that which is grasped cognitively are not identical, do not coincide.

As something which is demanded, recognition is dependent on a space in between opening up. It would however be an unacceptable simplification were this in-between space to be understood as a space which separates nature from culture and which can be added to the space of nature and the space of culture. If nature is externalized and culture is created, then nature and culture cannot be represented as two unities closed upon themselves or as two fixed poles kept apart by a certain distance. The in-between of recognition is not the in-between separating nature from culture, but the in-between which separates nature from nature and culture from culture. From such a point of view nature may be just a name given to the separation of culture from itself, to the in-between which transforms culture into something insecure, moving and teetering, into something multiple and varied, into something not-one and not-at-one with itself.

Recognition comes about because culture is never simply and entirely itself. Culture always means *between cultures*. This is why it raises the first demand for recognition. Each time something is recognized or is meant to be recognized, a recognition of culture is also at stake, between one culture and the other. Jean-Luc Nancy writes:

> Every culture is in itself 'multicultural', not only because there has always been a preceding acculturation and there has never been a simple and pure origin, but above all because the gesture of culture is one of mixing: there is competition and comparison, transformation and reinterpretation, taking apart and putting together differently, tinkering with and combining. (Nancy, 6)

The multiplication which results from the gesture of mixing Nancy defines as the gesture of culture, cannot be subordinated to a unity which holds the multiplicity and the mixture of cultures, gathering the mixed and multiple cultures in one single culture. Otherwise the in-between would be erased. The mixing would become a cleaning up, a figure of purge and purification.

The idea that culture is never simply itself, that it is not a unity or a unified entity which incorporates and comprehends deviations and aberrations as moments of its own development and differentiation, is an idea Freud unfolds in his text *Civilization and its Discontents* [*Das Unbehagen in der Kultur*]. In doing so, he regularly uses the words 'to recognize' and 'recognition', in such a way that the usage he makes of them reveals certain regularities which can become relevant for a conceptual analysis. At the beginning of his text, for instance, Freud maintains that one must take into consideration the 'discrepancies between people's thoughts and their actions' and the 'diversity of their wishful impulses' (Freud I, 64), if one wants to understand what it is that leads to the general recognition of a singular individual and his achievements. To the extent that whatever is to be recognized should not be severed from its appearance, to the extent that it requires recognition because it appears, to the extent that the difference between being and appearance introduces the difference between recognition and re-cognition, that which is to be recognized is not identical to itself or one with itself. Therefore, recognition never refers to the identity of an individual, it never refers to an identity which can be re-cognized and re-cognized again unambiguously. Recognition cannot be justified by pointing to clearly established criteria, by clearly stating criteria derived from an individual identity.

When Freud doubts that the oceanic feeling described by Romain Rolland as the origin and source of religion, is really 'to be recognized as "*fons et origo*" of the whole need for religion' (ibid., 65), he implicitly draws our attention to the fact that recognition becomes necessary when no unanimous decision can be reached about how to distinguish what is original from what is derived. One hypothesis may be more plausible than the other; it may be more convincing to seek the origin and the source of religion in a 'sense of guilt' belonging to the 'essence of culture and civilization', or to recognize the existence of a 'special, independent aggressive drive' (ibid., 118), a death drive or a destructive drive which 'works silently inside the organism towards its dissolution' and which for this very reason can hardly be proved to exist. Yet no certainty guarantees the unity of the object – if it exists, the death drive is 'alloyed'. The question of the origin of the religious need thus remains a question of interpretation. There is no unity conferred on the object which would allow us to be certain of it and to recognize it in its essence as a determinate object. Every argument which must begin or end with a recognition, its object never being identical, is therefore characterized by a *speculative moment* which Freud emphasizes time and again in order to secure the scientific accuracy of his procedure.

If one follows the necessarily speculative arguments Freud presents in his genealogy of religion and culture, one must suppose that recognition occurs for the first time when the opposition of ego and object takes the place occupied by the bond or the 'being-one with the universe'. In the beginning recognition is always a 'recognition of an "outside"' (ibid., 68). Yet this 'outside' reveals itself to be ambiguous and thus already something alien, foreign, threatening. It is both a source of pleasure and a source of displeasure.

There is no recognition in an undifferentiated being-one; there is no recognition without limitation, separation, isolation; there is no recognition without the possibility of making distinctions, without a prosthesis and a being-not-one. But whenever an ego has detached itself from an object, whenever it has been possible for such a detachment to occur, no closed unity, no permanent support has existed in the first place. Through the detachment which allows for the constitution of that which recognizes and that which can be recognized, the being-not-one manifests itself in the latter by transforming it into something which demands recognition. However, the being-not-one also manifests itself in the one who recognizes; it exposes his identity to an uncontrollable 'outside'. This 'outside' can appear in the form of an 'external authority' and prompt the 'recognition of the tension' (ibid., 136) which exists between the ego and the authority, a tension which can also be discerned in the authority recognized and in the recognizing ego, given that the suppression and the satisfaction of drives both depend on the relationship of the ego to an authority. The recognizing ego wears at least one prosthesis. For in that which is one, in the wholeness of the oceanic and the universal, there is no recognition, no ego which can confront an object and hence become a moving force, a vehicle, a bearer of culture.

If, then, Freud's usage of the concept of recognition in his essay on *Civilization and its Discontents* appears to confirm the insight that that which is recognized does not remain constant in its being or becoming, that it does not subsist as a merely natural entity and that for this reason it is something yet to be recognized, a perpetuated demand, one must ask oneself whether it is not possible to create a link between such a usage of the word and the understanding of culture which permeates the essay. Does Freud rely on the concept of recognition because culture is never simply itself and because it cannot reinstate a previous unity, the preceding being-one? Does he rely on it because one always moves between cultures, never just within one single culture?

To attempt a reconstruction of the cultural process Freud thematizes in his study, means to be tempted by an interpretation which considers this thematization to be part of the process itself, regarding it as a testimony to culture. Two questions arise at this point. Is it possible to find signs in Freud's essay which can be re-cognized as signs of culture? What is it that makes a text a testimony of culture, what is it that makes *Civilization and its Discontents* such a testimony?

15

The first question can be answered by pointing to two passages. In the beginning of his essay Freud mentions a letter he has received from a friend. This letter expresses thanks and critical praise for an earlier piece of work. The friend responds to the study on the *Future of an Illusion* which he has been sent by its author and reproaches him for failing to acknowledge the 'true source of religious sentiments', namely that 'oceanic feeling' whose immediacy and universality Freud ends up questioning. When referring to his friend, Freud does not name him: he leaves his name unmentioned. He is content with speaking of a widely recognized and 'exceptional' man. Freud does not even call his friend a friend, he does not openly and explicitly recognize him as a friend. Thus the reader is simply informed that the person referred to describes himself as a friend in his letters. When Freud speaks of the 'views expressed by the friend whom I so much honour', he can be understood as appropriating a designation used by the other. It is only in a footnote which he added to his text later on that the name of the friend is revealed. Freud says in the second edition of his essay that he no longer needs to conceal the name, intimating that in the meantime the letter-writer has himself included the originally private and confidential information in his own books and thereby rendered it public. Thus rather than immediately referring to the friendship and discussing the friend's argument in the light – or in the name – of a friendship based on mutual recognition, Freud chooses the discretion of a detour; he chooses a mediating elision which can doubtless be interpreted as a sign of a cultural achievement or of the 'high level of civilization or cultivation'. Freud is not afraid of the danger that the reader might confuse discretion with tacit reservation; he seeks to exclude this danger through the context, yet cannot completely avoid it, allowing the reader to be misled, at least for a moment, into the erroneousness, the deception or the disorientation of a perplexity or a suspicion. In doing so, Freud does justice to the friendship and the recognition of the other. Why? Because respect for a friend prescribes attentiveness to the distinction between the public and the private sphere; what remains unsaid in that which is said publicly indicates the attentiveness prescribed. But perhaps there is another reason why Freud does justice to the friendship and the recognition of the other; friends are sensitive to the being-not-one which determines recognition. They know that they will confer a destructive constancy and a dissolving solidity upon the discretion and the discreteness of their friendship the moment they invoke it. This is the aporia of friendship as a testimony of culture. Neither the strategy of omitting a name, marking the omission and putting recognition within quotation-marks ('he calls himself my friend in his letters'), nor the naive honesty of naming without hesitation and mediation can do justice to friendship unambiguously.

The second passage from Freud's essay to which one can point in order to answer the question of whether it is possible to find signs of culture and cultivation in the text itself, is contained in the fourth chapter. The 'recognition of love as one of the foundations of culture and civilization' is said to divert both the author and the reader, to lead them away or to distract them from the only relevant argument; however, this very diversion or distraction can serve the purpose of 'fill[ing] in a gap left in an earlier discussion' (ibid., 101). Thus the diversion or distraction has a methodological function, it serves the aim of creating an order. Freud recognizes the signs of order as those of culture, even if they are also to be detected in nature, in contrast to those of cleanliness. 'In none of my previous writing', Freud states, 'have I had so strong a feeling that what I am describing is common knowledge and that I am using up paper and ink and, in due course, the compositor's and printer's work and material

17

in order to expound things which are, in fact, self-evident' (ibid., 117). Are not the signs of the superfluous and the useless with which Freud punctuates his text, testimonies of culture, at least to the extent that 'culture is not exclusively taken up with what is useful'?

The fact that in his essay on the discontents inherent in culture Freud keeps testifying to the topic he discusses, culture and civilization, can certainly be explained by adducing a trivial reason: writing about culture must be a cultural achievement, a recognition of culture, of something into which one is necessarily embedded because of the loss of the originary being-one. At the same time, though, one can also assume that a culture which by definition is disunited, not-one, producing a discontent over which it has no control, desires and demands to be recognized. It is impossible to write on culture without responding to this desire, to the demand for recognition, and without reproducing it. *Civilization and its Discontents* is a prosthesis, as every text is; not every text alike, though, since not every text makes the disunity, the being-not-one of culture its object. Freud's concluding remarks, his vacillation between a revolutionary abolition of culture and a conservatism which holds on to the inevitability of the cultural evolution, can also be read in such a way that the prosthetic character of the text itself is discerned in these remarks. The essay is neither part of a culture whose unity it has restored prosthetically, nor is it an unrelated part, member or fragment which stands outside culture.

It is this indeterminacy which transforms a text – which transforms *Civilization and its Discontents* – into a testimony and a product of culture. But how does the indeterminacy of the prosthesis, of the cultural product and the testimony of culture manifest itself in a text? Its effects may become more evident if one considers a (trivial?) observation Lacan makes in the seminar he devoted to the ethics of psychoanalysis. Lacan is surprised that readers often misrecognize the true object of Freud's essay. He interprets this misrecognition or misunderstanding as a general difficulty rather than a specific one caused by *Civilization and its Discontents*. According to Lacan, the meaning of a printed text evaporates; it diminishes and vanishes, it gives vertigo and generates deception, as the hesitating Faust knew all too well. The text must therefore be awakened to new life and the reader's efforts must be directed to capturing the fleeting meaning (Lacan, 211). If culture were a closed unity; if it replaced the original unity, the 'being-one with the universe', with the total and uninterrupted immanence of a second nature; if it transformed itself into an absolute prosthesis, thus requiring no further prostheses, no recognition, then this evaporation of the meaning, which results in an almost incomprehensible misrecognition or misunderstanding, would be an epiphenomenon not worth worrying about. The meaning of a text would be immediately present to the mind. Or it could be comprehended by immediately recalling whatever had been written down. The misrecognition or the misunderstanding Lacan laments and at the same time recognizes as an inevitable peculiarity, is made possible by the being-not-one of culture. It is perhaps for this reason that the necessity of a recognition belongs to the conditions which make culture possible. Where recognition is necessarily demanded, the possibility of a misrecognition is given. Because there is no integral culture, it cannot be decided whether texts, products and testimonies of culture, contribute to its maintenance and subsistence or not. There is no culture, there is no interpreted and reconstructed text which corresponds to the picture Freud gives of psychical or mental life in an impossible analogy, in an analogy which seems to anticipate a short story by Borges or Calvino. When it has not been altered and disfigured by trauma or physiological

19

influences, psychical or mental life should resemble a city which maintains the sequences of its historical development in its spatial juxtaposition, not touching or changing them. On the one hand, then, the indeterminacy of a text can have the effect of a misrecognition, a misunderstanding and a forgetting, an opacity, an incomprehensibility and an evaporation of meaning; on the other hand, it can have the effect of bringing about efforts concerned with reviving and reconstructing the text, with recapturing its fleeting meaning, with unifying culture itself.

Partaking in the evolution of culture, *Civilization and its Discontents* is a prosthesis, a testimony which responds to the demand for recognition inherent in a disunited culture, in a culture which in itself is not-one with itself. The testimony can never become an integral part of culture; it cannot establish its integral actuality. Whether *Civilization and its Discontents* functions in the service of culture or not remains undecidable. One can recognize it as a cultural achievement, but one cannot re-cognize it as such. If the relationship of this text to the cultural process it thematizes can be comprehended in this way; if, when dealing with this text, the notion of recognition must be used in the way Freud himself uses it, then it is possible to posit that there is a link between the way in which culture is understood in this text and the way in which the concept of recognition which permeates it is being used, a link which has its origins in the idea of an essential disunity or being-not-one of culture.

How does Freud understand culture? As a disunity, a being-not-one to which one cannot attribute a determined and unambiguous meaning, given that it can both assist and impede cultural evolution. Freud writes that it is always possible to regard the cultural achievements of science and art as an aberration, and that such an evaluation can never be wholly avoided or simply rejected as an impertinent and unjustified evaluation; he thus points to the indeterminacy of the being-not-one of culture. Culture is an open movement traversed by tensions, a movement which consists of the cooperation and the opposition between the forces of Eros and Thanatos, of the life and death drives. For this reason, the order which is produced when culture comes about and which is distinctive of culture, is always only provisional, a temporary order; it is an order whose conservative aspect stands in conflict with the tendency towards expansion and unification residing in the erotic impulse. However, the compulsion to repeat is not pure and no regression to the state of a previously established order can be conceived. Conversely, the tendency towards expansion cannot renounce the ordering element and the constitution of higher unities and syntheses. Separated from each other and viewed in isolation, the conservatism of culture and its hyperbolical revolutions both terminate in its abolition. Such an observation is of course the result of an abstraction; it is made possible by culture, since one can neither presuppose an original lifelessness nor oppose death by hypostasizing the ongoing changes resulting from an undisturbed and uninhibited expansion. In *Beyond the Pleasure Principle*, Freud suggests that 'inanimate matter' must have been transformed into animate matter 'by the action of a force of whose nature we can form no conception' (Freud II, 38); the possibility of such a transformation must have been inscribed in whatever preceded life, whether one thinks of this transformation in terms of a mediated transition or in terms of an unmediated passage. Life and death are both not-one. It thus becomes evident that the cultural process or the evolution of culture has not simply destroyed and replaced an originary 'being-one with the universe'. Were this being-one completely unrelated to the being-not-one of culture, a cultural process, an evolution leading to culture could never have occurred.

If culture does not grow organically; if, as Freud tries to demonstrate, the cultural process is without a foreseeable outcome; if the being-not-one of culture divides its conservative, destructive and productive aspects, never allowing them to be simply themselves; if one must criticize the idea of a foreseeable outcome secured by the ideality of a regulative idea or the projection of a unifying horizon, as an anti-cultural misrecognition, rather than praising it for being a recognition of culture – then a pointed and elliptic remark Derrida makes in a footnote does indeed become comprehensible. This remark is meant to counter the argument which claims that deconstructive thinking remains caught up in an irreconcilable 'performative contradiction'. Derrida responds to the objection Apel and Habermas raise against his thought by stating that there would be no critique, no discussion, no communication, no progress in knowledge, no history of reason and no history at all, if one did not stand inside and outside an order, or if one were not embedded in a certain 'performative contradiction' and traversed by its tensions (Derrida I, 260). To the extent that culture is not-one and not-at-one with itself, to the extent that one stands within culture and outside culture, thus between cultures, one always does something different from what one says and one always says something different from what one does. The fact that one presents arguments and is engaged in a discursive search for truth does not change this strange situation. By hypostasizing a unified reason and elevating it to an ordering principle which establishes unity, an attempt is made to limit the effects of disunity, of being-not-one; however, such an attempt amounts to an eradication of culture. From this perspective it is misleading to appeal to a reconstruction of concepts, values and norms, and to discredit deconstructive thought for its excessive and irresponsible iconoclastic tendencies. Deconstruction is precisely a thought of culture. Therefore it sometimes seems to speak out in favour of political reformism, while on other occasions promoting a radicalized permanent revolution. The conservative, destructive and inventive aspects of culture, the aspects of a disunited culture which are split because a pure preservation and a pure destruction would immediately cancel themselves out, can be discerned in deconstruction.

It appears that Freud's conspicuously consistent usage of the concept of recognition can be connected with his understanding of culture. This connection can be made because the possibility of recognition must be sought in the disunity, the being-not-one of the one who recognizes and thus ultimately in the disunity, the being-not-one of culture itself. The insight into this particular connection can now lead to the more general question of whether recognition could not be used in various contexts as an anti-dogmatic concept directed against dogmatic and pre-critical hypostasization and totalizations, as a concept with a divided place, located between cultures, in the in-between of the order called culture. The *dogmatic* usage of the concept turns recognition into a result, a stabilized relationship which can no longer be destabilized by the being-not-one of the one recognizing and the one recognized, by the being-not-one of recognition itself; the *anti-dogmatic* usage of the concept marks the disunity, it does so each time anew and each time differently. To the extent that nothing can be re-cognized without its being somewhat dependent on historical and cultural mediation; to the extent that the being-not-one, which separates the one re-cognizing from that which he re-cognizes, affects both, the generalization of an anti-dogmatic usage of the concept of recognition can be extended to areas where one might at first consider it inappropriate. In its most general and most radical form, the question one encounters when attempting such a generalization is the following: *Is it possible to conceive of a* relationship – *a judgement, a re-cognition, a description, a communication, an evaluation, an act, without recognition?* If one recognizes this question as being a pertinent and meaningful question, one gathers how important the usage of the concept of recognition can be, how decisive the distinction between a dogmatic and an anti-dogmatic usage.

Let us recap. Recognition confirms and at the same time establishes the unity of that which is to be recognized, the identity of the one who claims it. Therefore recognition is not a simple act. It does not simply help someone to gain a voice, it does not simply provide someone with a voice. It does not form a lasting community of individuals who are recognized by the other individual when recognizing him and who recognize the other individual when being recognized by him. It itself needs recognition, it implicates itself within itself and opens itself up towards something other, towards an outside, unable to delimit and incorporate this openness. There are always different kinds of recognition, recognition is always different. It proves to be historical. Firstly, because something naturally given cannot demand recognition – recognition is a cultural achievement. Secondly, because recognition actively participates in the evolution of culture, generating history by seeking to establish an identity or a unity. Finally, because its openness exposes that which is to be recognized and recognition itself to an unforeseeable future. The identity that recognition is supposed to confirm and establish, is a non-identity; the transition from the contingency of that which is dispersed and isolated to the necessity of that which is universal, a transition meant to take place in and through recognition, is a detour, a wrong track. It thus becomes clear that the one who is recognized and recognition itself are not-one. Confirmation and establishment do not coincide in recognition; consequently, the one who is recognized does not coincide with himself either.

This also means that only if that which is to be recognized does not remain in the immediacy of its being given, only if a deviation separates it from its definiteness, its definition or its determination, can it ever be re-cognized or recognized as something to be recognized. The one who is to be recognized demands recognition; the one who recognizes responds to this demand and is therefore no more himself than the one who is to be recognized – he is no more himself than recognition is ever simply recognition, a unified concept which would allow us to refer to it as recognition itself. Recognition is always not-one, as are that which or the one who is to be recognized and that which or the one who does recognize. Whatever demands recognition must be justified: a ground and a reason for its existence must be provided. A ground must be found, a basis must be created upon which it can stand; a reason must be given which indicates why the demand for recognition has to be fulfilled, why it is legitimate for an entity to claim that it should be treated as a rightfully recognized group or individual. Every demand and every claim is characterized by an uncertainty that makes it difficult to justify recognition as a reasonable and intelligible act, an act well founded, and to secure the grounds for that which is to be recognized. Without uncertainty a demand could not even be raised. But uncertainty also bestows an unconditional aspect on every demand; as a consequence, every demand asks for an unconditional and unjustified answer. Whether a demand will be heard or whether it will go unheard, must remain uncertain, too. The possibility of going unheard brings recognition close to faith and testimony; it is a constitutive element of its success, given that there can be no success without it. Recognition, demanded or claimed, never fully succeeds, not even when it does succeed, not even when the one who recognizes proves capable of providing the most convincing justification for his act. In addition, it must remain uncertain in principle whether the one who recognizes is being deceived by the one who demands recognition, or whether he can actually take this demand seriously. Because one can only recognize that which is not-one and not-at-one with itself, because the demand for recognition contains the possibility and the impossibility of its own justification without, however, itself forming a unity, recognition and that which is to be recognized resist re-cognition and knowledge. That which is to be recognized cannot be fully transformed into an object of re-cognition, into an available object of knowledge. The act of recognizing does not follow any rules which, when properly applied, allow it to gain control over recognition. Therefore one cannot simply re-cognize that which is recognized, one cannot re-cognize it as such, repeatedly; recognizing is something which never simply takes place. But where does recognizing take place, if it never simply takes place? Not in the originary unity of first nature and not in the thoroughly determinate immanence of second nature, but between cultures, in the being-not-one of culture. One can thus maintain that the first demand for recognition must be sought in culture, in a culture which by definition is disparate, disunited, crooked, queer. The first demand for recognition is the demand of culture. Recognition is a prosthesis of culture, it serves its function and yet reveals itself to be a foreign body, a cultural achievement perpetuating the being-not-one of culture.

But how can culture possibly demand something? To speak of a demand of culture – is this not the result of an inadmissible transference that contributes little to clarifying the problem of recognition? Should one not begin with the premise that speaking of a demand for recognition is sensible and meaningful only in the realm of so-called intersubjectivity, not in other realms? Or should one not rather suspend all decisions that relegate the demand for recognition to a delimited realm in which one always already knows what it is that can be recognized? Would such a relegation not exclude what remains foreign, alien and heterogeneous in that which is to be recognized? Would it thereby not eradicate the difference between acknowledgement and cognition, between a recognition which is not-one and a recognition which implies the possibility of identifying something for what it is, repeatedly? Is recognition not something which is demanded in the name of an abstraction and ultimately in the name of truth itself, so that it can never clearly transpire where the demand is coming from and what it is recognition relates to? To say that others demand recognition is doubtless not the same as saying that an abstraction, a concept or an event are to be recognized. Yet in both cases recognition is a confirmation and an establishment of what is supposed to be recognized.

If one now wishes to take up what has been suggested above and make general use of the concept of recognition to denounce dogmatic hypostasizations and totalizations, it is necessary to touch upon the limits of cultural evolution, upon the limits which, given that culture is disunited and not-one, are discovered historically, and which, in presenting themselves historically, show the being-not-one of culture. Can one not interpret the attempt to make a general anti-dogmatic usage of the notion of recognition, an attempt which starts out from the being-not-one of culture and thus from the limits of cultural evolution, as implying a reinterpretation of the idea that philosophy grasps its own times conceptually? Does such a reinterpretation not consist in giving this idea a turn or a twist by which it is extricated from positive dialectics?

If philosophy is to grasp its own times in and through conceptual thought, it must start out from the extremes into which those times polarize themselves. Few thinkers in this century

27

have appropriated Hegel's definition of philosophy so uncompromisingly as did Adorno. The demand that philosophy must be conceived of as philosophy after Auschwitz or, to be more precise, that Auschwitz must be recognized as the vanishing point of a contradictory cultural process, seems to be informed by a radicalization of the Hegelian definition or determination, uncovering its limitations and its anachronism. What this radicalization invalidates, is the assumption of a final systematization and determinate unification of all philosophical efforts to grasp the times conceptually; what it invalidates, is the assumption of a totalizing comprehension of historical becoming. But what can one learn from the attempt to radicalize the idea of a conceptual grasp of the times, to radicalize it by uncovering its anachronism and recognizing Auschwitz as that extreme of the evolution of culture from which philosophy will have to start out in the future? *Above all*, one can learn that philosophical discourse, whose ideality and generality presuppose its independence from historical occurrences and contextual relations, an independence without which conceptual thought could not even evolve, must not hypostasize this independence. Otherwise it interrupts itself dogmatically, it cuts itself off from its own possibility, from the possibility of an intrusive and transformative critique, from the possibility of a new form of argumentation which cannot be inscribed into the ideality and generality of the concept as a mere modification and continuation of already recognized and prevalent forms. Every idea which is worth being called a new idea because it communicates different insights and because it communicates insights differently, demands recognition. It marks a caesura and a discontinuity in the discursive continuity, a chance for change and transformation, a blind spot one cannot remove with cognitive means, a vacant space to which one can only relate by recognizing it or not recognizing it.

Yet is it possible *not* to recognize something? Not to recognize something at all is as impossible as it is to recognize something fully, to achieve full recognition by bringing the moments of confirmation and establishment into line until they coincide. Whenever one relates to something, if only with divided or distracted attention, one has already recognized it. Doubtless for recognition to be recognition, i.e. a confirmation and an establishment, more is required than just the fact of relating to something. Thus it is possible not to recognize something, but in a realm, an area, a sphere which cannot be clearly outlined.

Perhaps only that thought which approaches a blind spot, a vacant space, a vanishing point without remaining unaffected by this movement, succeeds in opening up a new perspective. Perhaps thought must relate to a vanishing point of its time if it is to open up a new perspective. Perhaps the recognition of a vanishing point of time – of the philosopher's times – is the condition for thought succeeding in opening up a new perspective. Something about thought resembles a character in Hugo Santiago's film *Les autres*, who, struck by a terrible event, the suicide of a loved one, loses his established and fixed identity, experiencing unforeseen transformations which result in a last transformation, in a transformation without transformation. The one transformed enters a crowd in which he no longer is a transformed person, but just another passer-by. This transformation, a transformation which is not a transformation, does not express resignation. For if hope is given for the sake of those who are without hope, then hopelessness should not be confused with the opposite of hope; it should be regarded as the rescuing shelter of hope. *Whether thought can transform whatever befalls it, is an issue no less decisive for it than its ability to break through the solidification of whatever exists.* Perhaps it can only break through the existing and its solidification by transforming what befalls it. Does it then not

29

attain its utopia along the vanishing-line of such transformations? Does it not attain its utopia by revoking itself in a transformation of the transforming activity?

Thought that wants to be more than a reproduction and
imitation of what is already known and what has already been
recognized in the tradition, traces the vanishing-lines of its time.
It does so in order to touch the times' almost invisible, yet all
too obvious extremes and to recognize an unlikely possibility, a
barely measurable and almost imperceptible danger, a pain, an
enthusiasm, a devastation, an indifference, a stimulation, an ex-
citement, an idiosyncrasy, a disappointment, an accident, a love,
a despair, an exaggeration. It allows itself to be attracted by the
uncertain marking of a border, by a gathering and dispersing
zero-point which it both discovers and invents. Is this not the
reason why thinking recognition and thinking in terms of recognition always amounts to thinking *after...*, for instance after
Auschwitz or after Aids, if thinking after Aids means taking into
account the effects that the tendency described by a possible
coincidence of the certainty and the definiteness of death have
had on received modes of thinking and patterns of behaviour?

The name 'Auschwitz' points to the difference between that
which has been recognized and that which has been cognitively
identified: that which has been recognized is not of a conceptual
nature. The anti-dogmatic thought of recognition constantly
measures itself against the excessiveness of a name: the singularity of a proper name transcends all measures. Through recognition, thought is drawn into the polarity of concept and name
which cannot be objectified; at least not to the extent that the
poles themselves are split and that the concept is traversed by the
name and the name is traversed by the concept. Given that
Adorno's thought of the non-identical, explicitly conceived of as
a thought after Auschwitz, is located in the tension between

concept and name, between cognitive function and experience, between comparability and incommensurability, it can perhaps also be interpreted as an anti-dogmatic thought of recognition, despite the fact that Adorno never claimed the notion of recognition for negative dialectics. This is not to imply that that which is being recognized affirms itself in negative dialectics as something positive, and that thought celebrates the name. Through recognition thought seeks to attain the extreme against which it turns with undiminished effort. That philosophy after Auschwitz takes its point of departure from an impossible recognition of the 'uttermost extreme', an 'extremity which eludes the concept' (Adorno I, 365), cannot mean that it abandons itself to the blindness of the name, succumbing to the irreconcilability with experience indicated by the name 'Auschwitz'. Rather, forced into recognizing what the name would refer to if it still referred to something, philosophy draws the energy of opposing and resisting the 'uttermost extreme' from its very recognition. This is made perfectly clear by Adorno when he speaks of a thought which measures and which must measure itself against the uttermost extreme.

A thought which can be called a thought of recognition because it traces the vanishing-lines of the times and tries to extend them to the uttermost extreme, a thought which recognizes such an extreme as its point of departure and which is therefore embedded in the tension which exists between concept and name, has no way of conceptually reclaiming the decision in favour of a specific point of departure and a certain name; it cannot recuperate what has been decided by providing convincing reasons for the decision taken. Whatever point of departure this thought commits itself to and whatever name it chooses is ultimately contingent, admitting only of a retrospective judgement. Just like writers, philosophers must be *informers*, to quote the title of a book by Bret Easton Ellis, informers who report back from a post up front, a post they mark themselves without disposing of a map. Their report is philosophical to the extent that it is a conceptual construction; but this construction cannot posit itself as an absolute, for it depends on a recognition which affects all positing and all positions. One can state retrospectively that starting out with the idea of a philosophy after Auschwitz enabled Adorno to conceive of a negative dialectics, even if he had outlined its motives in lectures given in the early thirties. The subsequent establishment or institution of a historical continuity which secures the coherence of Adorno's thought and of the philosophical development to which it belongs, must not obscure or dissimulate the moment of contingency which lies in the recognizing gesture of a thought. The gesture is not, as philosophers sometimes assume, an aesthetic category not to be applied to philosophy. Rather, it is linked to the contingency of recognition, of a recognition which, when aiming at a vanishing point it fixes contingently and yet not illegitimately, can lead to the opening-up of a new perspective for thought.

Thus whoever investigates the relationship between recognition and thought encounters a paradox which he must either resolve or recognize. Thought relentlessly tries to render its discourse intelligible, its argumentation comprehensible and its ideas acceptable, but the opening-up of a perspective within which an acceptable idea, a comprehensible argumentation and an intelligible discourse can be developed, seems to depend upon the recognition of an irrevocable contingency, a contingency thought cannot sublate. It is decisive for thought to risk such a contingency, to call it into play, to make a bet on it; however, there is no certainty as to what it is thought should risk, as to which name it should make its impossible point of departure.

Does such an understanding of thought not cast some light on the reasons for which Adorno's thinking often appears as loose, as open and uncovered, as abrupt and opaque, at least when compared to the thinking of other philosophers? Generally, these aspects are dismissed as the result of an impenetrable, because confused, argumentation; or they are rejected as the result of an excessive concentration on style, an uncontrolled will to create a style of one's own. It is well known that Adorno himself attempted to provide an answer to the question of philosophical presentation by using terms such as constellation and configuration. A philosophical presentation described as constellation and configuration does not seek to reflect a closed, thoroughly articulated sequence of argumentation. It is hardly a coincidence that the text which deals explicitly with the necessity of turning to philosophy after Auschwitz, and which explicitly discusses the necessity for philosophy to measure itself against an uttermost extreme, an extreme named by a proper name, carries the title of a meditation. Beyond the obvious allusion to the philosophy of the subject or the egological tradition which extends from Descartes to Husserl, the recourse to the notion of meditating also refers to something which concerns the presentation. In an impressive passage from his response to Derrida's critique of his history of madness (*Madness and Civilization*), Michel Foucault attempts to give an account of meditating and distinguishes it from the idea of a closed sequence of philosophical argumentation. He describes it as a movement of thought which brings forth discursive events and comprehends a subject within it which is itself mobile and exposed to change. According to Foucault, the meditating subject is constantly changed by its own movement; it does not simply underlie it. It must take risks, it must test itself, it must let itself be tempted and tried.

To the extent that it meditates, the thinking subject does not already control itself or its train of thought (Foucault, 19). This description fits exactly the line of argument we encounter in the 'Meditations on Metaphysics' with which Adorno concludes his *Negative Dialectics*. His meditative thought, intrusive because it must measure itself against the uttermost extreme rather than remaining in contemplation, moves between concept and name, between recognition and re-cognition, in the being-not-one of re-cognition and in the being-not-one of the concept which are both marked by recognition and by the name, by the recognition of a name and by the naming character of recognition.

However, recognition is not universal. It is singular and different each time it occurs, a recognition affected by that which is to be recognized. In his 'Meditations on Metaphysics', Adorno does not reflect on Freud's critique of culture; what they have in common with this critique is the conceptual opposition between culture and barbarism, as well as the genealogical insight that culture rests on renouncing instincts and erecting an ideal of cleanliness and purity, thereby dangerously repressing the animal and somatic element. But while Freud thematizes the being-not-one of culture in general terms, Adorno's meditations revolve around the concept of a culture after Auschwitz and receive their desperate impulse from the recognition of this uttermost extreme. This is not to deny that the analyses Freud undertakes in the form of a critique of culture must also be viewed in the light of the sceptical question he adds to the very conclusion of his text in 1931. They then appear as being guided by an insight gained from a vanishing point of the times. However, Freud does not explicitly place these analyses in the context of the paradoxical and absolute discontinuity which separates the after from the before, and *therefore* exposes the before to the effects of the after without any protection. How does the after which allows us to discern a recognition affect the recognizing gesture itself? How does it do so if one follows Adorno's meditations, his observations on a philosophy and a culture after Auschwitz? Must not a recognizing thought, a thought which measures itself against that which it recognizes in order to resist it, pay the price of a justification through which it becomes guilty?

Adorno defines culture as 'objectification of the spirit' (Adorno I, 365) whose domination after Auschwitz must be considered as being 'absolutely evil'. Objectified in culture, spirit elevates itself above that which is alien to it, above the 'wretched physical existence'; culture's various domains and sections, 'philosophy, art and the enlightening sciences', make an emphatic claim for autarchy. Hence culture programs its triumph as its failure. Spirit abandons the life it is meant to inhale and gives it away to incineration: 'All culture after Auschwitz is trash, including its urgent critique' (ibid., 367). Yet one cannot conclude from such a statement and from such a state of things that one has to refuse culture after Auschwitz. Refusing culture amounts to directly supporting 'barbarism', a barbarism into which culture has turned despite all enlightenment. After Auschwitz the process triggered by the being-not-one of culture, its splitting into a repressive and an emancipatory form of enlightenment, has reached an extreme point at which it has become impossible to continue speaking of a being-not-one of culture. At the same time, one cannot simply stop speaking of such a being-not-one. Attempts to distinguish culture from barbarism, or to identify them as being the same, henceforth condemn themselves. The laborious separation of one culture from the other is already apologetic.

Culture can be disposed of because even its critique reveals itself to be marked by the traits of restoration. This assertion does not just promote barbarism. Whoever responds to a radicalized critique of culture, a critique of culture which questions itself, with such a suspicion, acts as if he had certainty as to what is barbarism and what is not – an ultimately barbaric thought. He argues in the name of a resurrected or restored culture. To say that culture can be disposed of, means that one cannot or should not invoke its name to defend its achievements, thus contributing to the restoration of a resurrected culture. It is therefore necessary to make a distinction between a cultural achievement which distances itself from itself, and a will to culture which insists on supporting a restored culture in order for this culture to manifest and affirm itself, at best after paying reparations and working through its past. When reading the reviews and articles of the cultural pages, be they pompous and self-assured, streamlined and balanced, or refined and conservative, one can still sense the difference. Adorno's philosophy is directed against culture because it is directed against its restoration 'after all that happened in its purview without any resistance being opposed to it'.

At this point one would be trying to ease one's conscience if one were to resort to the thought that the notion of culture in Adorno designates nothing but a more or less independent sphere of bourgeois society, a superstructure in which the alienated spirit turns into its own object, assuming the forms of art, literature, philosophy, science, and terminating in culture industry. Doubtless one can quote passages from the 'Meditations on Metaphysics' in order to justify such an interpretation. One can even refer to a lecture from the early fifties in which Adorno maintains that 'it is not yet common knowledge' in Germany 'that culture in the traditional sense is dead' – as if the liquidation of culture in Germany had somehow left it untouched, or as if culture had been altered and transformed only by the transition into culture industry which occurred 'in the rest of the world' (Adorno II, 23). But in advocating the validity of this interpretation and thereby attempting to limit the extent of Adorno's radical critique, one betrays the impulse which incites it and leads to its radicalization. The culture one can dispose of is not just the culture identified with a historical phenomenon, with the super-structure of bourgeois society. One can dispose of culture in general. Freud uses the word in this sense, too, in the sense of a movement which brings about a distance between the life of human beings and the life of their 'animal ancestors', creating institutions which serve to 'protect men against nature' and regulate their relations (Freud I, 89).

Those cultures which appear to be unaffected by the development which led to Auschwitz are also affected by the consequences it had and it still has for culture. All so-called multiculturalism must measure itself against the consequences of this development and against this development itself, unless it wishes to contribute to trivializing and playing down what happened. Even if it could be proved that only a specific kind of culture and only a specific cultural development could lead to Auschwitz, all culture after Auschwitz must take as its measure the fact that a specific type of culture and a specific cultural development provoked those events which have received the name of Auschwitz.

When thinking opens up a new perspective, it tends towards universality and generality. Whatever resists generalization and universalization must first measure itself against the consequences deriving from the uttermost extreme a thought has recognized. Because this extreme is a recognized one, or one that should be recognized, an impossible memory of thought, the generality and the universality reveal themselves to be only generalizations and universalizations. They must measure themselves against other recognitions, other generalizations and universalizations. Thus the thought of recognition is not a thought of universality and generality, it is rather a thought of generalizations and universalizations.

But does not the concept of recognition belong to those terms which have adopted the tone of a suspicious mightiness, does it not belong to those terms which, according to Adorno, are 'tinged from on high' and have no right to be used after Auschwitz, not without undergoing a transformation (Adorno I, 367)? Does it not smack of pomposity, of the puffed up, inflated, self-important pose of the parvenu, of the patronizing demeanour of adults? Should it not be assigned to the linguistic realm of repression, to the linguistic field constituted by words such as authority, respect, personality, public figure? Do not current attempts in social philosophy to use the concept in order to signify the creation of a bodily, spiritual, moral and societal 'integrity of human beings', unwittingly betray its relatedness to that very linguistic field or realm? To be sure, these attempts do not try to solidify social hierarchies or existing class relations. However, by sticking to the idea of an identity confirmed and established by recognition, by clinging to the seriousness of a unity which is never exposed to the irony of a gap or a crack by the double aspect of recognition, the fact that recognizing means to confirm *and* to establish, they faithfully perpetuate a scheme which is essential to the constitution of a repressive sphere of language, thought and action. They thus inherit the legacy of an usurpatory mightiness without altering and transforming it in its very essence.

If the concept of recognition is affected by each recognition of a vanishing point of the times and by each opening-up of a new perspective for thought, one must seek the transformations recognition undergoes and is capable of undergoing. A first clue to a recent transformation undergone by the concept of recognition might be found in Beckett's plays. In his essay on *Endgame*, a play to which he refers in his first meditation, Adorno affirms that Beckett's plays show how the dialectic of master and servant reaches its disruptive end. It does not result in a higher figure of consciousness, but swings to and fro ever more slowly until the pendulum comes to a standstill. There is probably no disputing that the relationship between Hamm and Clov, the two main characters in *Endgame*, can be described as the tired and exhausted relationship of master and servant. At the very beginning of the play, Hamm threatens to withhold food from Clov because the latter does not carry out the former's orders promptly. This threat is funny, for it cannot be much more than a gesture, a reminiscence, an echo by which one can gauge the distribution of roles but not the power of the one in command over the person in his service. Master and servant put on an act, they play master and servant, as if the one-sided and unequal recognition which constitutes their relationship had not led on to its own sublation, but rather to an exhaustion which only allows for a repetition of the rehearsed, leaving no additional room to move and act, an endgame instead of a result. Has the progression of dialectics been thwarted by an event, by an uttermost extreme which is not a 'temporal projection of the concept', by an extremity which cannot be determined as the location of a dialectical reversal and which keeps infinitely delaying all possible endings? Or does the effort of a dialectical progression prove to be itself nothing but a helpless and powerless attempt to bring the game to an end, so that the presentation can be comprehended as a presentation of truth and the utterances can be understood as manifestations of the mind's or the spirit's powers and abilities? Whatever answer one chooses to give, one will always have to interpret the play and the event called 'endgame' as presupposing a more or less implicit, more or less explicit recognition, a recognition which cannot be recuperated, a recognition which cannot become intelligible. One will always have to privilege such an interpretation, even if one debates the possibility of there being alternative answers to the question raised, and

39

maintains that the generalizing effect deriving from the recognition of an uttermost extreme necessarily involves the alternative, the either-or in an essential indeterminacy. Why does the endgame presuppose an irretrievable recognition? Because in order for the end to be postponed in a game or a play both finite and infinite, something must be presupposed which cannot be recuperated and which forces the game to be continued, the play to go on. This presupposition cannot be re-cognized, it cannot become intelligible, it can only be recognized and it has already been recognized by the players, no matter how deep the recognition has penetrated their consciousness or awareness. If the recognition were not the recognition of an uttermost extreme, if its presupposition were not irretrievable, the endgame would not be an endgame, it would be a cognizant termination, a re-cognizable coming-to-an-end, a completion in which beginning and end ultimately reveal themselves to be indifferent and interchangeable. As a postponement of the end which takes place in the end itself and which tears the end apart, the endgame is an event without an event, an uneventful happening brought about by the recognition of an uttermost extreme, not by the re-cognition of a final goal. Adorno's assertion that Beckett's characters no longer know how to die, hits the nail on the head.

What is at stake here is stated and shown by the usage made of language in the brief opening monologue of the play. Its first words, preceded by silent omission marks and thus already put last, are literally an endgame, suspended and ironically pushed to the point of indifference between speech and speechlessness, between exhausted and inexhaustible speech, between fire and ashes, as if they were informed by that musical gesture which finds its most extreme expression in the concentration and simplification of the short television play *Nacht und Träume*: 'Finished, it's finished, nearly finished, it must be nearly finished', says

Clov in a toneless voice, in a voice which, in the notes to his Berlin production, Beckett describes as being at the 'limits of audibility' (Beckett, 46). The end makes itself heard at the 'limits of audibility' because it is an end, yet an end without end, an end endlessly postponed and therefore indeterminate, an end which exhausts the voice and which for this reason allows and even forces it to touch upon its own limits, the 'limits of audibility'. Hamm's first lines, a speech interrupted by yawning which in the French version of the play has a comic aspect because of the retarding effects which menace its intelligibility, can be understood as mirroring the end with which the play begins – at least if one sticks to its French version. The repetition of the vowel 'a', in its very isolation, blurs the limits between the mere letter, the expressive sound and the meaningful word; it lets the speech drift away and undermines the grounds on which the hierarchical symbolism of the alphabet erects itself. Thus a delayed beginning corresponds to the delayed end. The beginning comes after an end which never comes; its continuous interruption brings about an end within itself, a discontinuity which prevents it from consistently asserting itself as the beginning.

In the endgame, the end inheres in the beginning. That the game goes on, that the playing doesn't end can be explained by pointing to the beginning which inheres in the end. Yet beginning and end do not meet in a unity. The players wait in vain for the parts to form a whole, for the single moments to constitute a unified and meaningful context, a coherent connectedness of life. Thus *Endgame* shows the limits of recognition; if recognition is not fully achieved, master and servant must enter a playful, distancing, destabilizing, unsettling relationship indicated by quotation marks. The question raised by the endgame is the following. When does recognition occur, when does recognizing turn into recognition, when do the externally established and therefore conventional signs which make it possible to discern recognition, allow us to speak of a recognizing relationship, of a relationship which is not set in quotation marks, preserving and protecting identity and integrity rather than burying them under their own ruins?

The recognition of an uttermost extreme brings about an end-game in which all recognition that aims at establishing an identity experiences an exhaustion of its driving force: the endgame repeatedly delays the instant recognizing turns into recognition. *Because recognizing is necessarily bound to external signs, to arrangements and conventions, to learning processes and attempts at interpretation, to pedagogy and hermeneutics, to politics and institutionalization, the place where recognizing is supposed to turn into the stable relationship of an achieved recognition proves to be the place where an endless delay keeps postponing the awaited event. This is the place of an almost pure obligation; in the end the obligation would succumb to its own powerlessness if only an ending could be anticipated and the tension alleviated, the tension which is produced by the relationship this obligation entertains with a disappointing and disappointed ability: temporal delay and spacing triggered by a fundamentally uncontrollable play of quotation marks.*

The end of the endgame, the achieved recognition, is death. Thus recognition requires this game, it requires the play which prevents recognizing from turning into recognition and which reduces the demand for recognition and its fulfilment to elements of a pragmatics serving no purpose but the prolongation of a self-referential happening. The players feel too old to acquire new habits, they cannot learn to use words differently, they cannot teach themselves other words. In what happens here, the relation to something other and different has become its own echo. Domination appears to be the ironic domination over this echo, a parody and a disenchantment of mightiness:

CLOV: What is there to keep me here?
HAMM: The dialogue.

(Beckett, 30)

Whenever one speaks of recognition, one speaks either of its abolition and thus of something different from the act of recognizing; or one speaks of something which never condenses into recognition, something which is always different from itself, something which never occurs where it occurs, something which exceeds itself and falls back behind itself, something which consists in this very disparateness and which does not have the consistency of an object intended and referred to by speech. The act of recognizing does not posit and assert itself. This is its discretion and discreteness. Recognizing resists the direct speech of philosophical discourse, of a discourse which objectifies, thematizes and argues. If there is a linguistic medium for recognizing, it must be the medium of indirect speech, of insinuation and suggestion, of reserve and cunning, of shame and irony, of reverence or respect for the mask, as in that line of the original English version of *Endgame* in which Hamm replies 'I feel a little queer' – a line Beckett altered at the request of an actor who felt uneasy about a possible allusion to the character's homosexuality (Beckett, 51). Obviously, indirect speech, insinuation, suggestion, cunning and irony can be means of a dissimulating and dissimulated self-assertion. They must be, at least to the extent that recognition is linked to a demand or a claim. But no self-assertion is able to find in the recognition of the other and in the other's recognizing act the stable grounds it needs in order to control the play of recognizing. No recognizing turns simply into recognition, thus asserting itself. To the objection that it is precisely the arbitrary and conventional character of recognizing which allows one to decide upon the external signs for its discernment and upon the usage made of its concept, one can respond by insisting on the fact that something conventionally established remains such only if it does not contribute to confusing a stabilization with a stability. It must mark its own conventionality and thereby draw attention to both the possibility of anchoring and the possibility of playing and changing.

A recognizing which never condenses into recognition and whose medium is an indirect speech which cannot be fully translated into direct speech, is particularly dependent on the singularity of a situation and a context, since the demand for recognition must be *each time* a demand for interpretation, for comprehension and explanation. In order to understand that a recognition is taking place, in order to explain which kind of recognition is occurring, why, how and between whom, the circumstances of the act of recognizing must be considered. Yet recognizing is also independent of specific contexts, given that it cannot be simply and immediately identified and determined. The re-cognition of the recognizing is overtaken by the recognizing itself.

If the recognizing has always overtaken its re-cognition; if the endgame, a play inseparable from recognizing, is programmed by the impossibility of re-cognizing a first principle and a final instance; if the concept of recognition is transformed by the endless flight of images in Beckett's play, a flight of images which does not produce an image; if it is transformed in such a way that the recognizing can no longer be thought of as a recognition, as something resulting at the end of an exhaustive process; if the exhaustion is made permanent in a world in which a servant who asks his master why he keeps him in his service, is told that there is no one else, an answer which prompts the ambiguous reply that there would be no other position to fill either – then one must raise the question whether a different world can be conceived of, a world different from the world defined in terms of recognizing. In the world defined in terms of recognizing, one circulates restlessly between cultures and their worlds, one is torn apart, thrown backwards and forwards between the impossible demand for recognition and the impossible fulfilment of this demand. In such a world, words barely have a meaning any more; the endgame, a playing with cultural trash, is endlessly repeated. An insecure, indefinitely floating net, an almost motionless surface which can hardly be distinguished from the depth underneath, signs of recognition exposing nothing but their flat exteriority, an apathy of slight excitements which cannot be attributed to anything, uncertainty of the smallest distance: the uttermost extreme of recognition, an exhaustion touching an ending and hence something which has transformed the recognizing relationship, something which is different, other.

THE CULTURE OF QUOTATION

What does recognition mean?

Confirmation and establishment constitute the double trait which distinguishes recognizing, which splits it up and exposes it, which creates the open relationship between heterogeneous moments within recognition itself. Because of this double trait, recognizing relates to itself, presupposes itself and projects itself into the future without ever being able to catch up with itself or to assemble itself in a unified act. Recognizing is not the solid ground of a recognition which allows the one who recognizes and the one who is recognized to lead a stable and continued existence. It is a relationship, a belonging-together of that which remains incompatible, of that which cannot be comprehended, of that which can never be grasped as forming a unity. It is a relationship of discreteness, a separating, im-pertinent belonging-together which interrupts its own unity. This impossible relationship through which the recognizing relates to itself, this self-reference which keeps referring to something else or to another, reproduces within the act of recognizing the relationship between that which recognizes and that which demands recognition. For that which recognizes relates to the other in such a way that the act of recognizing splits into a confirmation which amounts to a presupposition, and a projective establishment which amounts to an outlining of that which is to be recognized. Recognizing is a complex act because it is not-one with itself and because it is in need of itself. One could define recognition as *the need for a self* and as *the need of the self.* The self needs itself, it presupposes itself and exposes itself in order to catch up with its presupposition and to make up for its lack through recognition; through a recognition which must catch up with itself and its own lack. As an act which must be attributed to someone who is in need, the act of recognizing might be driven by the impetus of creating a complementary and completing mirror-image of the self. However, it does not have the force of leaving behind permanent traces, traces a self (the self of the one who recognizes or the self of the one who is recognized) can re-cognize repeatedly as its own traces, as traces allowing the self to be certain of itself.

The relationship between confirmation and establishment, which perpetuates the need of the self and the need for a self within the act of recognizing, is not a relationship of additive composition, as if an establishment were added to a confirmation and thereupon the one contrasted with the other. For whatever is to be confirmed is at the same time what the act of recognizing must yet establish. Nevertheless, the act of recognizing can only refer to that which is to be recognized, it can only refer to something or to someone other if a certain equality, a certain sameness and a certain homogeneity prevail between that which recognizes and that which is to be recognized. It is in this sense that one can speak of a confirming purpose and effect of the act of recognizing. But that which is to be recognized is also something other, something different, something which is other and different because it awaits an outstanding establishment it cannot simply regulate and control, something which is other and different because to demand recognition, it must be other and different. All recognition responds to a demand which marks the withdrawal of the other; all recognition responds to a demand by suspending the otherness of the other; all recognition surprises the other by establishing that which it recognizes, while at the same time letting itself be affected by the withdrawal of the other. That which is to be recognized does not know what will happen to it and what it will do to that which recognizes. Conversely, that which recognizes does not know what will occur to it and, because of its own response, to that which it recognizes. The act of recognizing is, to use Nietzsche's words, a *Ver-Änderung*, a change which effects otherness, not a *Ver-Ichlichung*, a change which produces the identity of a self; or better still: it is a *Ver-Ichlichung* only to the extent that it is also a *Ver-Änderung*, a *Ver-Änderung* which no self can bring to a standstill and which cannot be re-cognized repeatedly as a moment belonging to the subject's unity. Between the one who recognizes and the one who is recognized, equality and inequality, sameness and otherness, homogeneity and heterogeneity prevail. This tension characterizes the act of recognizing and distinguishes it from merely re-cognizing something or someone repeatedly.

The fact that the recognizing relationship is one of inconstancy and tension, both homogeneous and heterogeneous, symmetrical and asymmetrical, reciprocal and interrupted by a caesura, indicates its dependency on determinate contexts. The difference within the act of recognizing, a difference which cannot be sublated by the identity of a recognition, by the unity the act of recognizing is supposed to form when relating to itself, is each time a different difference, manifesting itself differently each time. It is a difference, a distinction that distinguishes itself from itself. Thus to recognize something or someone is always a repeated and multiple act, an act which occurs in many different ways; it is a being-not-one which is not-one, which on the one hand implies a certain conceptual unity and allows us to speak of an act of recognizing, of its discordant being-not-one, while on the other hand implying itself in the very practice of recognizing, in a practice of permanent *Ver-Änderung*, of a limited and yet unlimited multiplication of events. *If one wants to speak of an act of recognizing, one must assume a conceptual unity, however wild, and a struggle for the concept of recognition, for its conceptual unity and for the interpretation of the difference(s) which traverse the recognizing relationship; this struggle never ends, it is fundamentally interminable.* Choosing a traditional philosophical terminology, one can say that one must posit reason as the beginning of the understanding (Förster, passim) and at the same time think the beginning as divided by an uncontrollable arbitrariness and a radical contingency. There can only be a hermeneutics of recognition if the hermeneutic effort is not directed at the synthesizing idea of an ultimate horizon of interpretations, and if it recognizes the essential openness and multiplicity of horizons. There can only be an analytic of recognition if its elements are taken apart without the idea of a determining unity informing this process, and if the suspension and essential indeterminacy of such a unity are recognized. Yet how can one respond to the question of the meaning of recognition in a zone as turbulent as the one in which it must be raised?

Neither a naive inductionism which collects instances of the term in various contexts and seeks to derive the meaning of recognition from them, nor a dogmatic conceptual Platonism which hypostasizes essential traits of recognition, can provide an answer to the question. Inductionism falls prey to the bad infinity of the examples it collects, while conceptual Platonism ends up denying the usage of the term. With regard to its current use in social philosophy, one might say that conceptual Platonism isolates and totalizes the unity of the act: exempted from its being-not-one, the act of recognizing is expected to include this being-not-one within itself and thus to submit it to its unity. Consequently, to answer the question of the meaning of recognition is to describe a stabilized and generalized usage of this term or concept, rather than a stable and general one. But if one describes the act of recognizing as the open relationship between two irreconcilable moments, then it is impossible to assign the demand for recognition to the linguistic competence of the subject that is to be recognized. Something unavailable lies in the tension which marks the act of recognizing, something which transforms it into a demanded, assigned, commanded act, making it impossible to identify the demand, the assignment, the command, to trace it back completely to an instance of speech. The language in which the expression 'to recognize' or the notion of recognition is used must itself be considered to be a relationship between incompatible and incommensurable forces, between forces which have both a stabilizing and a destabilizing effect; therefore, such a language is reliant on an act of recognizing different from an act of re-cognizing repeatedly. Recognizing never exhausts itself in its linguistic mediation; the conceptual distinction between an act of recognizing and an act of re-cognizing repeatedly can be introduced only after the fact. *The speechlessness of the act of recognizing is that which remains immemorial about it, while making one speak.* Thus to emphasize an 'essential trait' or a 'logic' of recognition can only have the function of criticizing a particular usage of the term, a usage which, for reasons to be determined in each case, suppresses a decisive aspect of the habitual usage and encourages a conceptual confusion, a confusion affecting thought. Quoting a number of sentences in which the expression 'to recognize' is used in similar ways, whilst acknowledging that no contextual link relates these quotations to each other, can only serve the purpose of strengthening such a critique and of recalling the irrevocable contingency of language-games.

Frege's logical investigation on negation, published in 1919, begins with the following sentences:

> A propositional question contains a *demand* that we should either *recognize* [*anerkennen*] the truth of a thought, or reject it as false. [. . .] The answer to a question is an assertion based upon a judgement, whether the answer is affirmative or negative. (Frege I, 54 – emphasis A.G.D.)

Freud's psychoanalytical investigation of negation, published in 1925, ends with some general remarks on the function of a judgement:

> But the performance of the function of judgement is not made possible until the creation of the symbol of negation has endowed thinking with a first measure of freedom from the consequences of repression and, with it, from the compulsion of the pleasure principle. This view of negation fits in very well with the fact that, in analysis, we never discover a 'no' in the unconscious and that *recognition* [*Anerkennung*] of the unconscious on the part of the ego is expressed in a negative formula. There is no stronger evidence that we have been successful in our effort to uncover the unconscious than when the patient reacts to it with the words 'I didn't think that' or 'I would not (never) have thought of that'. (Freud III, 239 – emphasis A.G.D.)

Wittgenstein's notes on the concept of certainty, written between 1949 and 1951, contain an apodictic statement:

> Knowledge is in the end based on *recognition* [*Anerkennung*]. (Wittgenstein, 49 – emphasis A.G.D.)

In Austin's lectures on performative utterances or speech-acts, held in 1955, one can find a recognition of the possibility of violating the conventional rule on which the success of a performative utterance depends; this possibility is always given:

> For a procedure to be *accepted* involves more than for it merely to be the case that it is *in fact generally used*, even actually by the persons now concerned [. . .] It must remain in principle open for anyone to reject any procedure – or code of procedures – even one that he has already hitherto accepted. (Austin, 29)

Heidegger's meditations on the principle of identity, presented in 1957 at the University of Freiburg, refer to the idea of sameness in Parmenides' famous poem:

> He [Parmenides] places us before an enigma which we may not sidestep. We must *recognize* [*anerkennen*] the fact that in the earliest period of thinking, long before a principle of identity had been formulated, identity itself speaks out in a pronouncement which rules as follows: thinking and Being belong together in the same and by virtue of this same. (Heidegger I, 27 – emphasis A.G.D.)

In his essay *Redemption through Sin*, which appeared in 1937, Sholem explains the foundation and the development of the Sabbatian movement as arising from the necessity of making a decision:

> One had to choose: either one heard the voice of God in the sentence of history, or else one heard it in the newly revealed reality within the depths of the soul. 'Heretical' Sabbatianism

was the result of the refusal of large sections of the Jewish people to *recognize* [*anerkennen*]* the sentence of history by admitting that their own personal experience had been false and untrustworthy. (Sholem, 88 – emphasis A.G.D.)

As varied as the usage of the term recognition might be in this more or less arbitrary collection of passages; as difficult as it might prove to compare the implicit or explicit recourse to the concept which characterizes them; as much as one must recognize the disparity and the singularity of the arguments, of the theoretical and historical contexts in which they occur, at least if one wishes to do justice to the various ways in which the concept of recognition is used in the sentences quoted – these sentences and these passages still have more in common than the purely abstract and formal fact that a concept of recognition is expressly or tacitly appealed to in each one of them. For this fact itself manifests a certain 'necessity' which perhaps relates to an 'essential trait' of the concept of recognition, to a double aspect or trait that seems to be decisive for the thought of recognition and the

---

* When revising the present translation, I noticed that the phrase from Sholem quoted here does not include the verb 'to recognize' in its English version. Intrigued, and because of the relevance of the word's usage to my argument, I contacted the author of the German translation of *Redemption through Sin* to which I refer (1992), only to find out that the word Sholem uses in Hebrew cannot, strictly speaking, be translated as *anerkennen*. In Sholem's own German translation (1936–37), the verb *optieren* [to opt] is used to translate *le-hikana le-din ha-historia*. A literal translation would render this as 'to submit to the sentence of history'. Thus the English translation proves to be right. Rather than deleting the whole passage from my book, I have decided to keep it and to change the English translation whilst at the same time alerting the reader to the obvious mistake. I believe that the argument I try to develop does not simply depend on the actual occurrence of the term 'recognition'. Recognition translates, and translation recognizes. A.G.D. January 1999.

usage of the term, especially in the language-game in which a distinction is made between recognizing and re-cognizing repeatedly. A brief examination of the six passages can show this. But does the array of the quotations not denote a privileging selection, does it not attribute a preference or a 'special status' to philosophical texts and to that which Foucault calls the 'great interiority of philosophy'? Should the reader infer that the truth of recognition can be condensed into philosophy and that philosophy alone is capable of stating the truth about the discourses and practices of recognition? Four passages are taken from philosophical treatises or texts; thus one could quite legitimately stress the limitations imposed upon the selection. But whether restricting oneself to primarily philosophical texts betrays an objective adherence to a biased procedure, a submission of the topic to be discussed to a procedure which entails unrecognized presuppositions and which therefore must have significant consequences for the discussion of recognition, is not proved by merely pointing to limitations which undeniably determine the choice of quotations. After all, the examination of the passages in question is linked to the assertion of a fundamental openness that prohibits confusing the act of recognizing with a single unified concept allowing only for a single unified usage.

1. As regards Frege: If grasping a thought does not coincide with its truth or its untruth; if one can grasp a false thought; if the existence or the being of a thought does not consist in its being true, given that thinking (as 'scientific work' or as the 'work of science') is related to the possibility of untruth and thereby to the possibility of questions which in principle require an openness, a decision or a judgement on what is true and what is false; if false thoughts 'must be admitted [*anerkannt*], not indeed as true, but as sometimes indispensable' (Frege I, 37) to establishing the sense of interrogative sentences and ultimately to

making thoughts possible, the thoughts at work in such sentences; if, at the same time, truth and falsity of thoughts remain independent of any judgement and any recognition, so that only that which has being can be recognized and so that truth, that which has being, exists even if it is not recognized 'by any human being' (ibid., 42) – then one must conclude from the logical investigation of negation, in the course of which Frege grasps these thoughts about a thought and demands the recognition of their truth, that the concept of recognition is indispensable to the discourse of the logician, though he does not analyse its implications. It is indispensable to him because truth has to be disclosed by thought, rather than being immediately given. The resistance and the distance which separate the cognitive subject from truth and which are supposed not to affect it any more than falsity, leads to the conclusion that a recognizing and a rejecting belong to re-cognition, a recognizing of truth and a rejecting of falsity, of that which has falsely been recognized as true. The truth (of a re-cognizing thought) is not simply *re-cognized* by a judgement; above all it must be *recognized* by it. The act of judging is an act of recognizing; re-cognition, that in which thought, judgement and indication are linked together, is a recognition. Thus if one limits oneself to the usage Frege makes of the concept of recognition, the process of recognizing seems to imply a certain asymmetry, a certain imbalance, a certain heterogeneity between that which has being and cannot be altered, and that which is always open and temporal, a judgement or a decision. But it also implies a certain homogeneity: that which is recognized is something which is re-cognized, not something which in its very truth remains inaccessible, impenetrable, sealed.

It is this conclusion that matters here. One may, however, add a few questions directed at Frege's logical investigation. Must not false thoughts *always* be recognized as 'indispensable' if a thought is to emerge, if judgements on truth and falsity are to be passed? What does one 'grasp' – what does one 'grasp' when one 'grasps' a false thought? Does one 'grasp' a false thought? Does one ever recognize something as false, is it not always the truth or something taken for true that one recognizes, does not the false have the value of a negatively recognized truth, at least once it is recognized? Frege insists that truth and falsity remain what they are, regardless of all possible judgements: 'a false thought is still a thought' (ibid., 37), it is never affected by its negation, much less 'dissolved' or shattered. Yet what consistency does the false have if recognition is regularly the recognition of truth and if the false is a negative truth in which one can discern the truth and by means of which one can recognize it? Can the act of judging, which is supposed to have its proper place in logic, be reconciled with the act of taking something false for true, an act which, according to Frege, obeys 'psychological laws' (Frege II, 1)? If from a logical point of view one can conceive of false thoughts, but not of false judgements, must one then not analyse the judgement from a psychological point of view too, namely in all those cases in which one has won or conquered an environ- ment and ventures 'to judge about things in the external world', thus exposing oneself to the 'risk of error' (ibid., 23)? How exactly do these two points of view, these two possibilities of judging, relate to each another? Is it pertinent to maintain that the realm of thought, as the realm of true judgements, is the realm of the 'non-sensible' which enables us to recognize an external and an internal world, to conquer a dangerous environ- ment, an environment of false judgements (ibid., 27)? Does the indifference of truth with regard to the act of recognizing mean that recognition never simply establishes what is being recog- nized, that it is impossible to affect what is or what ought to be recognized and that within logic it makes little sense to speak of such a possible affection? Does it mean that whatever is being recognized can be affected only from a psychological point of view and that the 'work of science' or 'scientific work' as a logically pure grasping of thoughts, as a logically pure questioning which seeks to recognize their truth, is informed by the purpose of a pure recognition of the true? Is the fact *that* one must judge and recognize something 'merely external and psychological' in view of the judgement's relationship to truth (Adorno III, 286)?

2. As regards Freud: If one is not allowed to abstract from the function of judging and to pay attention to the content of a representation only, given that the repressed can be substituted by its negation or by a 'rejection' (Freud III, 236) and that consequently one can take some note of it, albeit not fully accept it; if the negative function of judging, the negation, effects a splitting up, a division of the repressed and thus its partial 'intellectual acceptance' (ibid., 236); if the negating ego, which recognizes the unconscious, enables the function of judging to come into its own precisely through the negation; if thereby it liberates itself from the compulsion of the pleasure principle, from the original affirmation, from the domination of the unconscious which knows of no judgement and which persists in a timelessness without contradiction, even though the repressed finds a substitute in negation and is able to penetrate into consciousness – then recognition once again reveals itself to be a process which on the one hand implies a certain asymmetry, a certain imbalance, a certain heterogeneity (consciousness, not being alien to the notions of time and contradiction, differs essentially from the unconscious), while on the other hand entailing a certain homogeneity: this homogeneity becomes manifest in the possibility of a (limited and restricted) suspension of the event or the movement of repression, in the possibility of a 'full intellectual

acceptance of the repressed' (ibid.). Freud's model of thought, a model which allows us to determine the negative function of judging and thus the function of judgement in general, evidences the fact that recognition (as negation) can reproduce *within itself* the resistance (of the repressed and the unconscious) caused by the moment of heterogeneity which is constitutive of it. This is why, as a process and a (part of an analytical) procedure, recognition can also be symptomatic.

3. As regards Wittgenstein: If thinking means doubting, and if a 'reasonable person' does not have certain doubts (Wittgenstein, 29) because endless doubting can no longer be called doubting (ibid., 58–9); if knowledge is an 'assurance or a certainty which has calmed down' [*beruhigte Sicherheit*], rather than being one which is 'still struggling' (ibid., 46); if knowledge, the 'assurance or certainty which has calmed down', represents a 'form of life', and if to live means to be content with 'some things' (ibid., 44); if, not unlike life or forms of life, language-games just 'stand there' without rational justification (ibid., 73) – then (rational) knowledge and the assurance it guarantees must be grounded on a recognition which does not presuppose doubts leading to the re-cognition of reasons and which is not based on the re-cognition of legitimating grounds; it must be grounded on a recognition which, resulting from a struggle for assured reasons and at the same time rendering such a struggle possible in the first place, establishes or institutionalizes language-games as 'forms of life', language-games which remain in principle unforeseeable. As with Frege and Freud, the concept of recognition Wittgenstein resorts to in a decisive passage is marked by a double trait and a necessary tension. The recognition indispensable to a justified and securely grounded knowledge is a recognition of reasons to be rendered only to the extent that it recognizes the impossibility of an integral rendering of reasons, the impossibility of a self-

grounding of rational thought. Thus the act of recognizing is characterized by the asymmetry, the imbalance, the heterogeneity of an immeasurable, groundless relation, *and* by the homogeneity existing between reasons rendered or re-cognized and their possible (rational) recognition. A thought guided by reason and reflecting on rationality cannot provide itself with its own ground or foundation and thereby come to stand on it; it cannot 'stand there' fully justified; thus it requires recognition and takes on the more or less sharply contoured form of a 'form of life', into which it is also embedded. In contrast to Frege's logical investigations, recognition is not added to a truth which maintains itself in absolute independence of the recognizing judgement. Here, recognition precedes all re-cognition and all judgements, for it is their very possibility. It is almost impossible to affect it, to touch upon it and alter it. *At the same time*, however, it exposes itself to an altering affection, much more so than any judgement and any re-cognition ever do.

4. As regards Austin: If, from a linguistic perspective, the act of recognizing is a performative utterance, and if, conversely, the recognition of conventions must be counted amongst the essential general conditions of any complete performative utterance (Austin I, 14); if, as a consequence, it is always possible to reject, revoke or suspend conventions and the participation in speech-acts, given that any regulation of such acts already refers to an originary, pre-conventional recognition of conventionality which cannot be classified as pertaining to performative utterances – then, assuming one is willing to reconstruct Austin's argument and its implications in this way, the concept of recognition that can be formed and developed in the course of such a reconstruction designates both an opening-up and a confirming assertion of that which has been opened up. Once more we find that recognition must be thought of as a movement whose opposite

poles create a tension. A certain asymmetry, a certain imbalance, a certain heterogeneity which are produced by the difference between a convention which has not yet been established and a convention which has already been established, are as constitutive of the act of recognizing as is a certain homogeneity, a homogeneity created by the opening-up of a space and the inauguration of a temporal sequence, which both allow for conventions to exist. This means that the act of recognizing does nothing but outline itself and project itself into the future, and that it can be revoked at any time without the revocation being justified.

5. As regards Heidegger: If one must recognize something where something reveals itself ('identity itself speaks out'), where one cannot sidestep an evidence which triggers the desire to sidestep it, precisely because it is inseparable from an enigmatic, concealed, non-evident aspect – then the one who recognizes is caught up in the inextricable tangle of a homogeneity and a heterogeneity. Recognition proves to be unavoidable, as it were; that which is to be recognized keeps avoiding or sidestepping any possible insight, it keeps conditioning the reflex, which in turn tries to sidestep it. We are thus faced with the symmetry and the similarity of the dissimilar and the asymmetrical, with the restraint of a generosity, with the miserliness of an abandonment, with the withdrawal of a presence, with the controlling of an exposure, with the fascination with an otherness that traverses the same, with the expropriating event of the same's belonging, with the impertinence of pertinence.

6. As regards Sholem: If a cleft can open up between inner experience and external history; if the conflict arising from the divergence of differing realities forces a decision and a recognition, given that any reality ultimately depends on the unity formed by the internal and the external and that it is therefore necessary to hold on to both realities; if the borders which separate the

internal from the external become permeable because of the recognition required by the contradiction, so that the external and
the internal constantly keep changing places and one is drawn
into a spiral of paradoxes, into a chain reaction which produces
paradoxical situations; if apostasy, the 'paradox of a fallen Re-
deemer' (Sholem, 88), testifies to the paradoxical consequences
which derive from the recognition of an 'inner experience', and
offers the unforgettable spectacle of 'a dialectical explosion of
new forces in the midst of old concepts' (ibid., 97) – then recognition, understood in the sense of Sholem's presentation of
Sabbatianism, is caused by the tension a deviation of history
creates. History constitutes and deconstitutes itself by deviating
from itself, by being not-one and not-at-one with itself, by failing to be a unified teleological tendency leading to a goal. Inner
and outer experience, political and spiritual life, reality and idea,
facticity and validity do not coincide, nor do they simply complement each other. They are divergent and even antagonistic
forces, urging a decision which cannot rely on a coherent and
transparent knowledge, since it results from a contradiction and
generates paradoxes. Thus recognition proves to be a radical
historical occurrence, something which happens between a certain asymmetry, a certain imbalance, a certain heterogeneity that
separates experience from itself and redoubles it, and a certain
homogeneity that is to be sought in the attempt at overcoming
the separation by means of paradoxes.

It is hardly a coincidence that the explicit or implicit recourse
to the concept of recognition in the examined passages, in passages taken from works on psychoanalysis, logic, ontology, the
philosophy of language and the history of religion, time and
again leads the train of thought to where the relationship to
something else, something other, something not immediately
given or present (the unconscious, truth, knowledge, history,

conventions) is a tense one, a relationship marked by a tension extending between sameness and otherness, homogeneity and heterogeneity, balance and imbalance, symmetry and asymmetry. If one wished to define recognition as a pure relationship of otherness, then one would not be in a position to explain how it is possible to relate to the other without a moment of sameness; if, conversely, one wished to define recognition as a pure relationship of sameness, then one would not be in a position to explain how it is possible to relate to the same without a moment of otherness. Finally, if one wished to define the relationship between sameness and otherness as a purely dialectical one, recognition becoming the conceptual epitome of a positive dialectic, then one would not be in a position to answer the question of what it is that distinguishes a recognition resulting from the sublation of otherness from a recognition, from that knowing-oneself-in-the-other that sub-lates difference and the non-identical in the unity of an identity, and that, rather than requiring or needing recognition, already comprises it within itself.

Recognition is neither a state of affairs nor a result. It never simply belongs to truth, it is never just false or untrue, it never appears as an 'assurance or a certainty which has calmed down', an act normalized by conventions and norms, or by a historical teleology. With striking regularity, recognition reveals itself to be a contradictory movement, charged with tensions, divided and disunited within itself, a movement which cancels out all attempts at determining an unambiguous and simple relationship to truth, to consciousness, to knowledge, to conventions and norms, to teleologies and eschatologies, regardless of how we conceive of such relations.

One can say that that which has been recognized was in need of recognition and yet remained indifferent to it. One can say that recognition exposes itself to being affected and altered and yet resists altering affections: it can be affected in its very resistance to affections and it resists affections in its very exposure to them. One can say that recognition is divided by the otherness of that which is recognized and yet refers to an other whose dominance it thwarts. One can show that, on the one hand, recognition precedes itself and rebelliously escapes all determinations and fixations, while on the other hand allowing itself to be fixed and determined conventionally. One can detect in the act of recognizing that which cannot be sidestepped, that which, being unavoidable, triggers the desire to sidestep it. One can emphasize the radically historical character of recognition and still interpret this radical historicity as an overcoming of history . . . It thus belongs to the concept of recognition to withdraw from an integral conceptual determination. A struggle for recognition does arise and must arise. Why? Because recognition is in itself polemical, given its essential indeterminacy. What Derrida calls a 'structural unconscious' blocks the constitution of a self-consciousness through recognition. Everyone who believes to have been fully recognized keeps declaring in utter astonishment never to have thought that such a thing could happen to him or her. The struggle for recognition does not come from outside, it is not added to recognition externally; rather, it inhabits recognition and is perpetuated by the act of recognizing time and again. Therefore, no recognition can be conceived of, which would be able to put an end to the struggle for recognition and transform the insecurity and uncertainty that it effects into a secure ground or foundation. Since each attempt to grasp recognition conceptually and to determine it as such without ambiguity – be it in terms of an insurmountable otherness, an established identity, or a re-cognizable teleological process which comes to an end once its goal has been reached – is doomed to failure, one can always form more than just one, just *a single* concept of recognition. The conceptual effort that tries to turn the act of recognizing into an object it can thematize and objectify, remains submitted to a never-ending struggle for recognition: it is always already involved and entangled in such a struggle. Even 'its' difference, the difference of recognition, is the 'difference of its ways and its modes [*Weisen*]' (Menke I, 90), without it ever being possible to affiliate these ways and these modes beyond all doubt. Each way and mode is also something other than a way and a mode, something other than a tune [*Weise*] which can be re-cognized: there is a dissonance here which can no longer be measured against a consonance, a how which transcends every why, a *modus* without foundation, a pure 'who whom?'. *Recognition remains bound up in a struggle for recognition, in a polemic.* This struggle (the word 'struggle' is no less suspect than the concept of recognition itself, for it is saturated with the pathos of the existential, 'tinged from on high' by the exaltation of the heroic) never comes to an end by recognition being transformed into a result, into a stable and permanent being-recognized; it comes to an end only when one touches the limit of recognition and experiences its exhaustion.

Hyphens

If in order to speak of an act of recognition one must presuppose the precarious unity of a concept whose synthesis cannot fully and completely grasp the ways and modes of recognizing, then the question arises as to how the general and the singular, the universal and the particular relate to each other in the struggle for recognition. In what sense can one speak of a universality of recognition? One can speak of a universality of recognition in the sense of an overarching and unifying trait or characteristic which makes it possible to repeatedly re-cognize recognition in cases and instances each time different. Such a repeated re-cognition can rely on formal criteria or on criteria of content which are used regardless of the specificity of the cases and instances of recognition, allowing for an 'effective' act of recognizing with a relevant and meaningful content to set itself against a merely 'formal' recognition, to give but one example. The overarching and unifying trait or characteristic, the trait or the characteristic of universality, makes recognition transcend the particularity and the limitation of its specific ways and modes. One can also speak of a universality of recognition in the sense of formal and content-based criteria which are valid only in a particular domain, in a single context within which specific ways and modes of recognizing claim validity. The universality one speaks of is then the generality one attributes to the different contexts; it endows the ways and modes of recognizing with their unity in each of these contexts.

How one uses the verb 'to recognize' depends on how one conceives of the relationship between universality and particularity which characterizes recognition. It depends on whether one conceives of it in terms which dissimulate the tension which distinguishes recognition from a repeated re-cognition, or whether one conceives of it in terms which maintain and recognize this very tension. Universalism seems to be the most appropriate notion to designate the first approach. For to privilege the universal is to subordinate the tension which permeates recognition; it is to submit the difference which traverses recognition, and which is in turn traversed by a difference, to an overarching and unifying feature. The price universalism pays for this subordination and this submission is an implicit or explicit dissolution of recognition into a repeated re-cognition. Every act of recognizing which, in the end, remains bound up with a superordinate instance of universality is unable to affirm its difference when referring to or resorting to such an instance. It is unable to affirm the difference which marks each one of the many and various ways and modes of recognizing another or something other. If it were to affirm its difference, the universal instance would not be a superordinate instance; it would not be capable of assimilating the difference and would thus expose itself to it.

In his *Tanner Lecture*, Michael Walzer draws a distinction between 'two kinds of universalism', between the universalism of an encompassing, covering law and the universalism of a reiteration which is not guided by any law that could be exempted from its reiteration. The concept of recognition plays an essential role in this context. It is not just an example used to illustrate the effects which the preference given to one of the two kinds of universalism has on the relationship between heterogeneous cultures. The positing of principles which claim universality beyond the specificity and singularity of cultural contexts, and which constitute a precondition for the constitution of such contexts, requires a general or universal recognition if the multiplicity of cultures and the diversity which exists within each culture are not to be obfuscated. Everybody re-cognizes himself or herself repeatedly in the preceding principles he or she recognizes. Walzer, who advocates a reiterative universalism, a universalism consisting of repetitions which are not preceded by any principle or universal instance, must oppose such a concept of recognition which in truth is a concept of repeated re-cognition, he must set a different concept against it, a concept which does justice to the relevance and significance of reiterations, to the fact that a principle can never be recognized without being affected and altered by its recognition. No principle can be recognized without its fundamental character being robbed of its certain grounds. From the point of view of a reiterative universalism, there can be neither universal principles nor a general and universal recognition. Universal principles require a general and universal recognition, but this recognition or this acknowledgement reveals itself to be a repeated re-cognition. 'Acknowledgment is additive and inductive', says Walzer (Walzer I, 527). One never recognizes or acknowledges something or someone from an 'external standpoint' or from a 'universal perspective'. In other words, each recognition of universal principles which leaves them untouched and remains subordinate to them has already relinquished its singularity, the singularity of a different and heterogeneous cultural context which is different and heterogeneous in itself. It has already abandoned itself, as it were, given that it is always a singularity that asks for recognition, that demands it. *Universal and preceding principles can only be recognized from the external standpoint of a universal perspective, but precisely for this reason they can never be recognized – they can only be re-cognized repeatedly or posited dogmatically.* How does Walzer conceive of the relationship between the particular and the universal? Does he intend to resist the dissolution of recognition, the eradication or sublation of difference, by means of a reiterative universalism? What is it that makes reiterative universalism a universalism; what is it that makes the reiteration a reiteration which cannot be fully understood and grasped from a universal perspective? How exactly is a reiterative universalism different from the universalism of an encompassing and 'covering' law?

Reiterative universalism is supposed to recognize the 'local intensities', the 'particular forms', 'the pluralizing tendencies' – in short: the difference which marks cultural contexts and the difference which exists within such contexts. It is supposed to do so without intention and result diverging, i.e. without otherness, heterogeneity and difference becoming themselves a principle that endows recognition with certainty because it precedes the act of recognizing, an act reiterated time and again and thus always different. By assuming a stance against the universality of a preceding principle, a stance which is twofold given that it is directed against both the principle of universality and the principle of difference, reiterative universalism attempts to resist the indifference of recognition which paralyses reiteration, at least if reiteration is meant to be 'an ongoing and controversial activity'. Walzer writes:

> Indeed, it is always possible [. . .] that we will be overwhelmed by the sheer heterogeneity of human life and surrender all belief in the relevance of our own history for anyone else. And if our history is irrelevant to them, so will theirs be to us. We retreat to inwardness and disinterest. Acknowledging difference makes for indifference. (ibid., 515)

Walzer's assertion that recognition can produce indifference does not imply that one should dissolve difference in a preceding and superordinate unity, or that one should dissolve heterogeneity in homogeneity and singularity in universality. However, the transformation of difference into a recognized and repeatedly re-cognized principle which produces indifference and causes a retreat into the domesticity of an allegedly untouched interiority, can be interpreted as a reaction-formation caused by the overwhelming violence which may erupt from difference. This means that nothing safeguards reiterative universalism from the universalism of a principle, that nothing protects recognition from a repeated re-cognition which erases it. Yet precisely because the experience of difference, of the 'sheer heterogeneity of human life' can overwhelm the one who tries to recognize something or someone, provoking a reaction-formation or an apotropaic recognition; precisely because the possibility of a universalism of the 'covering law' or of general principles is contained in reiterative universalism – can the act of recognizing be stronger than a repeated re-cognition and reiterative universalism prove to be more resistant than the universalism of the 'covering law'. This strength and this resistance derive from the very powerlessness of reiterative universalism, from *the weakness and exposure* of the act of recognizing.

The recognition of difference could not produce indifference if the contexts, cultures and histories were entirely disparate and unrelated to each other; the fact that something or someone is being recognized points to a relationship, regardless of the ways in which someone or something is actually recognized, regardless of the function and the effect a specific act of recognizing may have. Perhaps the overwhelming aspect of an experience of difference can be explained by referring to the impossibility of establishing a relationship which holds difference in an equilibrium.

69

It is impossible to establish a balancing relationship between the relation to another history, another culture, another context and the unrelatedness which interrupts this relationship. Thus the relationship which exists between cultures cannot be described as a relationship which creates a universal culture, a unified teleological history, a meta-context, or which legitimates the presupposition of such a culture, such a history, such a meta-context. Rather, this relationship – which is also an interruption, an unrelatedness – has to be thought as an iteration or a repetition and as an iterated iteration or a repeated repetition, as a reiteration which has to take place again and again and which is always more than a simple repetition of something already given and established. Each time it takes place, the repetition is also an alteration and a transformation; *as* a repetition it has an altering and transforming effect. Without this effect one could not explain the case of philosophers who of their own accord and in the name of the professional recognition they have received, in the name of their reputation as defendants of reason and truth, in the name of recognized guiding principles of argumentation and a re-cognizable erudition, take the initiative of writing an open letter to protest against the academic honours bestowed on another philosopher, a philosopher who in their own eyes should not be recognized as a philosopher. Without the altering and transforming effect of repetition, one could not explain the conflict between different ways and modes of recognizing. One could not explain the case of philosophers who in the name of their professorial duty to the state exclude students from universities and refuse to recognize them as students because they are unwilling to fight for the fatherland in distant and foreign wars.

A recognition which is meant to have no other consistency and no other content than the content and the consistency it is provided with by reiterations, both foreseeable and unforeseeable, may cause indifference. However, reiterations also create difference (ibid., 525). For a reader who takes this assertion of Walzer's seriously, it perhaps indicates that modification and alteration belong to the concept of an iteration, of a repetition. *Each single repetition must, as such, affect that which it repeats, even if only in a barely noticeable and almost irrelevant way.* That which is being repeated thus reveals itself to be more than just something which is being repeated. It is also different and other, it is also something unique and unrepeatable which can appear only in the repetition, in the division of the repetition, in the necessity to repeat the repetition. Repetition proves to be similar to the act of recognizing in that it is an open, not a closed activity. It is an activity that is not one or that is at odds with itself, that keeps reproducing itself and in its very reproduction produces a difference which thwarts both that which is being repeated and the repetition, that which is being recognized and the recognition.

Doubtless one must take into account the cohesive force of those socially significant factors which ensure the unification of repeated recognition and which support a regulated social behaviour. In his book *Spheres of Justice*, Walzer names rank, title, background, money and political power (Walzer II, 250). Doubtless social recognition often depends on socially determined prejudices, not just on the autonomy of those who recognize others, and is in fact strengthened by such a dependency. Doubtless it is important to distinguish between the repetitions and reiterations which occur within given and relatively stable cultural contexts and those which occur between different cultural contexts and which establish different cultural contexts in the first place. However, the disparity of cultural contexts is brought about by the very alterations and displacements whose inconspicuous, preliminary and uncertain symptoms can be gauged from the reiterations

71

incessantly occurring within unities almost closed upon themselves and contexts tightly knit. With each new reiteration or repetition, the cohesive force of socially relevant factors and socially determined prejudices is put to the test and must prove itself. The modifying aspect of repetitions is thematized by Kierkegaard in the following paradoxical statement:

> What is repeated has been, otherwise it could not be repeated, but precisely the fact that it has been gives to repetition the character of novelty. (Kierkegaard I, 34)

Even where the identity of that which is being repeated is supposed to be guaranteed by a repeated repetition; even where a repeated repetition is supposed to allow for it to remain self-same; even where repetition is meant to serve the ideality of an encompassing and covering law; even where it is at the disposal of a universalism – an unforeseeable and unpredictable element of modification and alteration intervenes which does not leave the ideality untouched. For this element of modification and alteration can only be repeated and idealized by exposing it to another unforeseeable and unpredictable element of modification and alteration. Do such considerations which we do not find in Walzer support his argument that reiteration creates difference? Do they justify his plea for a form of inductionism which alone can do justice to a repeated and always modified usage of the concept of recognition, of a concept without a stable conceptual unity?

Because no repetition can be (repeatedly) re-cognized as such; because every reiteration has to be recognized; because without repeatability or reiterability nothing could be experienced – it is possible to generalize the usage of a concept of recognition different from a concept of (repeated) re-cognition, the usage of a

concept traversed by the irreducible tension which exists between a homogeneity and a heterogeneity. Not only every new
and every renewed usage of the concept of recognition demands
recognition, but also every single repetition or reiteration which
establishes a new cultural context. Conversely, every act of recognition demands a repetition, a reiteration, since it has both a
stabilizing and a destabilizing effect, and since, not being a mere
object of exchange which is accepted or given away (Walzer II,
255), it is insignificant and remains worthless without a ratification and a reiteration.

Once the emphasis is put on that trait of a reiteration which
can be described as a more or less calculable, more or less anarchic creation of difference, a difficulty arises for any thought
which does not wish to renounce a claim to universalism. Reiterative universalism wants to strengthen cultural singularities and
to preserve the traditions of particular communities, but it seems
to lead to a loosening of geopolitical moorings and a dispersal of
historical legacies. Living in a world of reiterations which do not
form a whole, a world culture, living in a world which consists of
transitions, means basically that one lives in an in-between. The
in-between withdraws from attempts to objectify it; it is a blind
spot which can be justified only in retrospect, so that every
justification can be denounced as being an ideology. The generic
name given to such an ideology is *multiculturalism*. One can say,
for example, that the belated justification of a work of art is
ideological if it points to its multicultural value in order to praise
a content-based enrichment and suggest a political virulence.
The fact that an artist uses elements from various and differing
cultures does not yet mean that multiculturalism is involved in
his activity, no matter how painstaking the analysis. This is not
to imply that the artist appropriates the foreign and alien elements, that he manipulates or falsifies them, that he shows no

genuine interest in that which is foreign and alien. Rather, the reason why multiculturalism is not involved in his activity derives from the impossibility of objectifying the in-between as a representative intersection of cultures. *One cannot form another culture from the in-between; the in-between is the not-oneness of culture, as it were, its openness.* The artist or the writer finds himself in the position described by Roland Barthes at the beginning of his book, *The Empire of Signs.* The foreign culture transports the writer into a position of writing. Thus writing does not reproduce or represent the foreign culture (Barthes, 4).

The political dimension of the impossibility of objectifying the in-between as a representative intersection of cultures is roughly outlined by the example just given. While the ideology of multiculturalism promotes (political, legal, institutional) representation at the intersection of cultures, thereby perpetuating the suspicion of a manipulation and falsification of what it represents, a politics which refuses to continue serving such an ideology lets itself be transported into the realm of the in-between by the experience of the alien and foreign. This realm is neither the realm of the same and the self's own nor the realm of the other and the unfamiliar, it is neither the realm of a synthesis nor the realm of an opposition.

It is precisely because the unmistakable and distinctive features of a culture can appear only in a movement of transition, by virtue of a reiteration which modifies them already, that a reiterative universalism cannot be appropriated as an argument in favour of the cohesion of closed communities, or taken as an argument in favour of the dissolution of particular and singular cultures within an encompassing super-culture. Walzer's *Tanner Lecture* does not supply a radically communitarian argument, and even less so a radically universalist argument. The radicality of the thought of incessant reiterations resides in the fact that a repetition which necessarily requires another repetition is unable to play a merely confirming or a purely mediating role. Such a repetition, such a reiteration can no longer be grasped and determined with concepts of universality and particularity – they do not confirm the particular as such, as a figure of the universal. *Reiterations present us with the paradox of an irreducible and hence originary or preceding in-between, of an in-between which cannot be delimited by that which it separates and brings together – between cultures.*

Differences arise through or in an in-between. But only an in-between which does not presuppose what is different, and which can be distinguished and differentiated, is really an in-between and not just an objectification or a reification which supplements what can be distinguished and differentiated as something to be distinguished and differentiated in turn. Would it be possible to distinguish between cultures and create a link between a (contextual) inside and a (contextual) outside, if the in-between indicated the difference between an already constituted inside and an already constituted outside? Would it be possible to distinguish between contexts and cultures, between their respective inside and their respective outside, if the in-between formed a presupposition which could itself be identified as something different, as something distinguished from something else? Would it be possible to conceive of the constitution of an inside and an outside? Are inside and outside not solidifications which in their relative autonomy and independence refer to the in-between as the element, the medium or the middle of their constitution and differentiation, of their formation and divergence? Is the in-between as middle or medium not without a middle or a medium, is it not without a unity, so that it can only play a systemic role if it is predetermined and if its predetermination presupposes already what it is meant to predetermine?

Opposing the exclusive self-satisfaction and the oppressive expansionism of cultures, multiculturalism reminds us of the foreign and the alien within the familiar, within the domesticity of one's own home. It reminds us of the right to exist of other independent cultures. To the extent that this reminder, both a complaint and a demand, remains linked to the idea of a representation in the intersection of cultures, to a need for recognition which is to be satisfied by the means of representation, it holds on to solidifications, to aspects which have become autonomous, rather than exposing them as solidifications, as aspects which have become autonomous – as autonomous elements which do not presuppose a divided substance, but which belong to a medium without presupposition, to a middle without a middle, to an originary in-between. Even when referring to the extreme case of an inside which cannot be related to an outside because it consists of an absolute eradication, and of an outside which is eradicated by the void, the invisibility, the incomprehensibility of the inside, it is necessary, as Shoshana Felman points out, to create a link, a relationship between inside and outside – a relationship which engages both in an unpredictable, unknown, deranged and deranging movement, in a movement which thwarts the representation of the inside and the outside in a determined and determinable middle. What is at stake here is the impossible simultaneity of an inside and an outside which no representation is capable of transforming into a possible and regulated simultaneity; what is at stake here is the in-between of a testimony, an in-between as established in the film *Shoah*, an in-between in which this film tries to maintain itself; what is at stake here is a dialogue which cannot lead to an understanding, given that its absolute belatedness nullifies or destroys any objectifiable content; what is at stake here is, as Giorgio Agamben puts it (Agamben I, 33), something completely different from a bridging dialogue:

I would suggest that the impossible position and the testimonial effort of the film as a whole is to be, precisely, neither simply inside nor simply outside, but paradoxically, both inside and outside: to create a connection that did not exist during the war and does not exist today between the inside and the outside – to set them both in motion and in dialogue with one another. (Felman I, 232)

The act of recognizing must be reiterated, it must be repeated again and again, it must again and again create a new context, a new link, a new relationship, a new connection because neither the inside nor the outside (of a culture, of an event) can be self-sufficient, can be entirely transparent or opaque. However, each time the act of recognizing is repeated or reiterated, it is a different act since the in-between of the context or the connection it creates is each time the in-between of a new context or connection. When repeated, recognition is altered – even in those cases in which the repetition is designed to guarantee the stability and permanence, the endurance of what remains self-same. As a movement of the in-between, of the uncertain, unstable and ultimately indeterminable connection between the inside and the outside, the movement of recognition is an altering repetition and a repeated alteration. If one wished to understand the expression 'between cultures' as an abbreviated or cryptic imperative, it would oddly prescribe the impossibility of catching up with something, of bringing it back, and would read: *Stay in the gap of an in-between, keep creating new connections and forging new contexts!*

A repetition which alters what it repeats and which therefore is not just a repetition of something, a repetition which does not coincide with itself and which therefore creates an in-between space within itself, can under no circumstances occur between a

given universality and a particular which has become autonomous, mediating between one and the other or placing both in
an abstract juxtaposition. A reiterated act of recognizing cannot
be comprehended in terms of a general or universal recognition
which by virtue of its unity covers different and always singular
ways or modes of recognizing. One would misunderstand the
idea of a radicalized reiteration if one were to regard every reiteration as the sum of communitarian and universalistic elements.
Also, a reiteration does not mediate between the particularity of
a contingent historical identity and the universality of a rational
identity which sublates the historical and transforms the contingent into a determinate moment. The reiteration of recognition
thus reveals itself to be fundamentally incompatible with the
universalism of transcendental pragmatics. For such a pragmatics, identity is split into the contingency of an identity marked
by a specific culture and particular tradition, hence dependent
on a given context, and the necessity of a post-conventional
rational identity. If identity is essentially a split identity, the task
of transcendental pragmatics consists in reuniting the two identities in the unity of an essential and undivided identity, of an
identity which has caught up with itself, as it were. Because the
universalism of transcendental pragmatics as the universalism of
a 'covering law' encounters the difficulty of discerning possibilities which will allow for the reunification of a divided identity, it
exposes itself to the danger of falling prey to the effects of ultra-
nationalism. The division of identity assumes different forms; its
historicity stems from the fact that not every relationship between a rational and a cultural identity can have the same form.
Certain relationships must be privileged, at least from the perspective of a transcendental and pragmatic universalism, since
they are better suited to a mediation between the two identities
which relate to each other historically. The distinctive features of

a historical relationship between rational and cultural identity can thus always reflect the distinctiveness of a privilege; there is always an instance in which distinctiveness is nothing but the result of an unavoidable privileging. The philosophical ultra-nationalism one finds for example in the thought of Karl-Otto Apel follows from the universalism of transcendental pragmatics, and should not be considered as a regrettable and external addition to it. 'In 1945 everything was altogether different', Apel states in a conversation. He then says:

> At that time, we [the German people] had experienced a defeat of our national conceptions of life which – this is something I must repeat again and again – *was unique in world history*. I believe that the one who would be able to think this through to its ultimate conclusion, would have the opportunity of entering the realm of the post-conventional; he could do so *as a philosopher* and with a radicality which everyone else in the world must lack. (Apel, 38 – emphasis A.G.D.)

The ultra-nationalism involved in such declarations is obvious. Never were the German people less German, never were they more universalistic and more philosophical, never were they closer to the truth than at the time they were more German than ever. Apel recognizes the 'dangerous' implications of his thoughts, ironically pointing to the fact that he only 'secretly' holds the view presented. This view is made public as an unreasonable truth, as a truth one cannot handle too carefully and hence as a truth not everybody can handle, as a truth which has the character of a privilege and which therefore prompts a confession, an avowal, a declaration of belief and a proclamation of allegiance. However, Apel's recognition and irony do not affect the necessity inherent in his transcendental and pragmatic approach, for it is this approach itself which forces him to unfold his arguments the way he does, with a genuine or a compulsory will to consistency.

The universalism of transcendental pragmatics, which coincides with the universalism of a 'covering law' to the extent that it subordinates the particular to the universality of a principle and to the extent that the recognition of a contingent historical identity is meant to come into its own when this identity recognizes itself in a cosmopolitan identity based on reason, must solve the problem of how to mediate between the two identities, of how to bring back the particular identity to a universal identity. Yet if the relationship between the particular identity and the universal identity differs historically, if a particular relationship between the particular identity and the universal identity proves to be better suited for the purposes of a mediation or a bringing back, then it is inevitable that the universalism of transcendental pragmatics or the universalism of the 'covering law' generates a philosophical ultra-nationalism, a nationalism which recognizes the particularity of a culture, a tradition, a community only because it clears the way to a repeated re-cognition of the universal. On the one hand, such a universalism dissolves recognition in a repeated re-cognition; on the other hand, it gives repeated re-cognition the name of the particular which clears the way to it. It implicitly demands a universal recognition of the particular in which all can re-cognize themselves repeatedly, and which nevertheless must remain singular, a recognized singularity allowing for a repeated re-cognition. Who if not a German, a German philosopher who transforms philosophy and conceives of a transcendental pragmatics, is in a position to give an account of the world historical uniqueness Apel refers to, the uniqueness of the experience undergone by the German people? Who if not a German philosopher is in a position to think it through to 'its ultimate conclusion' and to provide the world with an ultimate philosophical grounding? A universalism which comprehends and determines the particular is always also a political particularism.

The consequence to be drawn from a reiterative universalism can be formulated in the following terms: the more a culture insists on its particularity and uniqueness, on its singularity, the more directly it exposes itself to another culture and the more it tends to merge into another culture. What, then, constitutes the universality of cultural reiterations whose unlimited perpetuation Walzer advocates? How is such a universality different from the universality inherent in a 'covering law'? It is the demand for a new and different reiteration, for the repeated establishment of new and different contexts of life and culture that Walzer calls universal. If the reiteration is multiple within itself and not a unified act, each single reiteration entails already the possibility of, and indeed the demand for, new and different reiterations or repetitions. No reiteration, no repetition, no demand for a reiteration can ever be adequate. The demand for a new and different repetition is never given as an abstract commandment or imperative; it is given only in the very movement of repeating and reiterating, in the recognition of the essential openness and multiplicity of all repetitions and reiterations, a recognition which takes place in the movement of repeating and reiterating and which therefore must itself be repeated and reiterated. Walzer speaks of a 'warrant for reiteration' which does not 'pre-exist every reiterative effort' (Walzer I, 527) and which in fact cannot even be a 'warrant'. *That* reiterations must take place and *that* each reiteration or repetition must measure itself against the transformed conditions which it creates and which it exposes to further transformations and repetitions, makes reiteration 'universal', even if the term universalism seems misleading here. Would it not be more appropriate to use this term in order to designate the claims to validity raised by and under a 'covering law'? The *that* itself must put itself to the test, prove itself again and again. Thus, Walzer does not posit universality as the universality of an essence, of a what. He seeks universality in the *that*, in existence. For this reason, it does not assume the form of an abstract commandment or imperative, but rather the form of an experience, a praxis, an act of recognizing or acknowledging. 'The experience of reiteration makes it possible, at least, for people to acknowledge the diversity of claims' (ibid.), Walzer writes, drawing our attention to the fact that an irreducibly *practical dimension* is inherent to recognition. As praxis, as an act, recognition is idiosyncratic and resists universality. To seek universality in the *that* does not amount to an ontologization or a dehistoricization of existence; on the contrary, it amounts to providing a space for praxis and history, a space whose delimitation must be preliminary, an interrupted demarcation, between a reiteration and the limited warrant which grants reiterations. Can we not interpret the irreducibility of praxis in the act of recognizing as its constitutive theoretical lack, as an impossibility to make the being-not-one enter the conceptual unity of an achieved and successful recognition? Can we not interpret it as the disparity of heterogeneous moments, as the difference which traverses recognition and which can never be sublated? The praxis of recognition proves to be a praxis precisely because it cannot lead to a result, to a recognition entirely re-cognizable by theory, and because it therefore cannot be fully controlled by conventions and regulations, by rules and norms.

One might be tempted to dismiss interpretations of a reiterative universalism which prompt such conclusions and which appear to open up the frame of Walzer's lecture as mere over-interpretations. Does Walzer not hesitate between a universalistic version of reiterative universalism and a way of thinking no longer guided by the opposition or the universally determinable difference between universality and particularity? *On the one hand*, he opposes the idea of a 'universal history' to the idea of a 'series of histories' which resist integration into the universality of a single history: 'universal history' reveals itself to be the fiction of a 'meta-narrative', as Lyotard would have put it. *On the other hand*, Walzer weakens the strength of the opposition and mitigates the violence of the irreconcilability which resides in the distinction he makes. Without clearly distinguishing his own argument from the exposition of an existing argument, he recognizes the possibility that all histories 'converge at the mythical end of time' (ibid., 514). *On the one hand*, he answers the question of universalism by conceiving of the unity and omnipotence which in Jewish monotheism are particular to God's name, as intrinsically plural; *on the other hand*, he wishes to limit the 'plurality of divine names', presenting it as a mere effect of finitude: the productive power of the human being appears as a 'reflected, distributed and particularized' divine omnipotence (ibid., 518). It is possible to criticize the somehow blurred character of Walzer's presentation, the undeniable vacillation which transforms his argument into an uncertain and unstable one, as signs of a dependence on the universalism of the 'covering law'. Perhaps, though, it is also possible to consider the lack of clarity as evidence of the radical uncertainty and indeterminacy implied in the idea of an unlimited reiteration, of an acknowledgement or a recognition whose conceptual unity cannot be extrapolated from the modifying movement of reiteration. It is not the undecidedness which hesitates between two kinds of universalism that should be regarded as proof of such an uncertainty and such an indeterminacy, but the possibility of an indifference produced by the recognition of a difference, a possibility inscribed in every reiteration. As a possibility which cannot be separated from the possibility of a recognizing reiteration and of a reiteration of recognition, it is itself indeterminate and remains indistinguishable from the other possibility, to which it cannot be subordinated.

Yet can one not give a different account of the indifference towards difference and recognition which is brought about by recognition itself? Can one not understand it differently than in terms of a simple reaction formation and a hypostasization of difference? Can one not understand it in terms of the limit-experience of an exhaustion of recognition, since reiterative universalism makes recognition necessary by demanding it time and again? From the perspective that this question opens up, the deconstruction of universalism which is a thought and a praxis of recognition and of unlimited reiteration must not inevitably trigger the 'fanaticism' of an 'intransigent tracing' (Habermas I, 187). A release and a letting-be may manifest themselves in such a thought and such a praxis.

The fact that we can find signs of a deconstruction of universalism in Walzer's attempt to think a universalism of reiteration, and that the deconstruction at issue does not terminate in a relativism or a contextualism, encourages us to turn our attention to Derrida's more or less systematic analysis of the concept or non-concept of iterability. How does this analysis affect the problems to be faced when dealing with recognition? Derrida introduces the concept or non-concept of iterability in his paper 'Signature Event Context'. Delivered in the late sixties at a conference on communication, this paper begins with considerations which in retrospect seem to anticipate the basic assumptions of discourse ethics. However, Derrida's arguments are propelled by the problematic implications of those assumptions and do not pursue the aim of making them into their own justified starting- and end-point. To the extent that current debates around multiculturalism tend to join the banner of a politics of recognition inspired by hermeneutics and discourse ethics, it is worth reconstructing the concept or non-concept of iterability in the light of the considerations Derrida presents at the beginning of his paper. The assumption of a horizon of communication, which serves as an orientation mark for all those who participate in the process of argumentation, belongs to the pragmatic pre-suppositions of the context within which the paper stands, as Derrida points out. Whoever communicates by exposing an argument, whoever wishes to communicate something by means of an argument, for example an idea about the possibility and impossibility of communication, finds himself already in a domain surrounded by the 'horizon of an intelligibility and a truth of sense'. This truth is necessarily a consensually based truth, for the one who communicates by means of an argument ultimately strives to produce a universal or 'general agreement', a concurrence which amounts to a justified and not only factual fulfilment of the claims associated with his argument (Derrida IIa, 3). Facticity and validity are meant to coincide when the communication which occurs in the course of presenting, discussing, criticizing and modifying arguments reaches its goal, a goal which, according to its own conceptual determination, it has kept approaching. From such a perspective, the impossibility of communication must always be subordinated to its possibility, regardless of the difficulties which must be overcome in the process of communicating. Derrida does not deny that this basic assumption belongs to argumentative communication, to a connecting and gathering communicative action, but he does have doubts as to the necessity of recognizing it as a basic assumption which cannot be questioned. For in order to be content with it and let it dictate the direction and the guiding lines of an argumentation which deals with the act of arguing and communicating, as discourse ethics does, it would be necessary to show that the diversity of contexts, which mark arguments and allow for arguments to emerge, can actually be sublated in a meta-context, in the unity of a universal, non-natural language which guarantees unified meanings and a unified sense or direction. If we follow Derrida, a radical and unifying decontextualization remains unthinkable. Because there can never be a determining meta-context, because a context can never be fully determined as a unity, because the fleeting of meaning and sense can never come to a standstill and meaning and sense can never be captured by a meta-context, one must think communication and argumentation in terms which are different from the terms imposed by the idea of a consensus which is to be established universally. It is precisely at this point that the concept or non-concept of iterability intervenes in the discussion. Thus the deconstruction of a consensual universalism does not dispute or deny its basic assumptions, it does not contradict them by opposing other basic assumptions to them; rather, it places them in a space or inserts them in a movement they can no longer control, since this space or this movement cannot be controlled by any basic assumption. This explains why the counter-argument often used by transcendental pragmatics or discourse ethics, the argument of a performative contradiction, can under no circumstances be regarded as a pertinent and valid argument against deconstruction. It always presupposes the possibility of a unifying meta- or zero-context in which the claims to truth made in various and varying contexts have been fulfilled. Because the predetermination of communication, of argumentation, of discourse cannot simply be transformed into a certainty, it is not a simple predetermination. The idea of iterability, whose rudiments at least are contained in Walzer's conception of a recognizing repetition and a repeated recognition, can serve to reveal the necessary limitations of a politics of recognition which aims for the establishment of a universal consensus. Only the one who tries to trace this idea, this thought, can gauge the political consequences of a politics of recognition.

How does Derrida develop the idea of iterability? He understands iterability to be the repeatability and changeability of a sign without which no communication could take place. In order for it to be possible at all, communication must remain independent of the presence and intention of the one who communicates; it must remain independent of its immediate contextual inscription; the possibility of communicating something must remain linked to the possibility of repeating it in the form of a quote. Far-reaching consequences can be drawn from these premises. An act of communication constituted and persisting independently of the one who communicates relates to particular contexts, since it is always at a certain point in time and within a certain context that something is communicated; however, it can never be fully determined in any given context. Because the intelligibility of communication is secured only by the fact that it must be repeatable in contexts which are each time different, that which is being communicated is exposed to a changeability which transforms its intelligibility into an always precarious and partial intelligibility. Only a meta-context in whose midst all possible contexts would be anchored could ensure that all the changes, to which each act of communication and each linguistic sign are susceptible from the very moment of their constitution, might be determined as mere modifications and integrated into an ultimately unchangeable unity of communication. Only the absolute context of a private or a meta-language could guarantee the identity of a linguistic sign and the self-reference of a communication; only such a context could make possible the creation of an unaltered transparency of the linguistic sign, thus opening up the prospect of the creation of an ultimate and final

accord which would prevent the act of communication, the communicated message, the one who communicates and the one to
whom the communicated message is addressed, to diverge from
each other. Only a context which in fact is not a context because
it either excludes or includes all possible contexts (a pure private
language and a pure meta-language coincide) could provide for
the dissolution of recognition into a repeated re-cognition. Does
the openness of contexts not demand a recognition which can
never be discerned within a specific context, but only between
contexts, in the in-between of contexts and cultures in which
nothing can be discerned? The in-between is not a space com-
parable to the spaces whose limits or borders it forms. Where does
something belong that moves in an in-between? *The belonging of
that which moves in an in-between is as uncertain as the belonging
of the in-between itself.* When Derrida writes that every element
which is subject to iterability must in some way remain repeatedly re-cognizable, one can interpret this repeated re-cognition
as a recognition, as a behaviour which relates to that which
withdraws precisely because it itself is not-one. An active translation of the sentence 'A travers les variations empiriques du ton,
de la voix, etc., [. . .] il faut pouvoir *reconnaître* l'identité [. . .]
d'une forme signifiante' (Derrida IIb, 31 – emphasis A.G.D.)
would render it as follows: 'Through empirical variations of tone,
voice, etc., [. . .] it must be possible to *acknowledge* [*anerkennen*]
the identity [. . .] of a signifying form.' Iterability is the name for
a double not-being-one: it is a name for the not-being-one of a
repetition entailing change, and it is a name for the not-being-
one of a change entailing repetition. Recognition is triggered by
iterability: the repetition which is not-one because it is also a
transformation; because it requires recognition and can lead only
to a recognition, not to a repeated re-cognition. But iterability is
also a name for recognition: as a relationship between a repeti-

tion which is never simply a repetition and a change which is never simply a change, it corresponds exactly to the open, not-unified movement of recognition, to the unruly and uncontrollable relationship between a homogeneity which is never simply a homogeneity, and a heterogeneity which is never simply a heterogeneity.

For this reason, the three conclusions Derrida draws from the notion of iterability can be transferred to the notion of recognition. 1) Just as there can be no purely private or purely secret language because language as language must remain independent of the speaker and his intention, there can be no purely secret pact between the one who recognizes and the one who is to be recognized, no conspiracy of the chosen few which would prove immune to the adversities of the common. The ones who recognize and the ones who are to be recognized can never place themselves in a position which would allow them to bring the movement of recognition to the standstill of a result. 2) Just as the consciousness or the awareness of the freedom of the speaker and the responsibility which such a freedom entails can never be instances of an ultimate control over language, one cannot apply a concept of responsibility to recognition which is based on the free will in the self-consciousness or self-awareness of the ones who recognize. This impossibility accounts for the possibility of both the radical negativity of the subversive Donjuanism analysed by Shoshana Felman and the experience which, according to Derrida, dictates a different kind of responsibility: the experience of an insoluble undecidability between the conditionality of contexts of which the ones who speak and the ones who recognize have a relative overview, and the unconditionality which announces itself in the 'opening and openness of every context' (Derrida IIa, 152) and which must remain an absolute challenge for the ones who recognize and the ones who speak. The intermittent character of intentionality has the effect of tying us even closer to our own speech, to our own (recognizing) behaviour, and of increasing our responsibility for our (recognizing) behaviour, for everything we say. There is no responsibility without a secret, an ellipsis, a withdrawal. 3) Just as the act of communication and the communicated message can never be fully determined within a given or an extended context, a phenomenology of recognition which determines its figures or manifestations in distinct and delimited contexts cannot turn the recognizing movement(s) into a determining concept. It follows from the fundamental openness of contexts that the meaning of a sentence which is conveyed by an act of communication cannot be determined exhaustively, and that every single word already attracts all the possible meanings of the sentences into which it could be integrated (Derrida I, 116). But if we understand the fundamental openness of contexts as the openness of a recognizing movement or of a movement of recognition, it also follows from it that gestures, utterances and ways of behaving can be interpreted as acts of recognition even before they acquire a repeatedly re-cognizable meaning within a syntax of recognition, and that no exhaustive syntactic order exists which allows us to attribute the meaning of an achieved recognition to gestures, utterances and ways of behaving.

If, following a suggestion we find in Apel's analysis of the implications of an interminable and eventful 'temporal play', one wished to gain control over the iterability of recognition by inscribing it in the frame of a meta-context and transforming it into a limited and temporary movement or into a movement of mere differentiation; if, under such circumstances, one wished to attribute to a particular context the function of paving the way to the meta-context and preparing the ground for its disclosure – it would still prove necessary to explain how the movement of recognition which occurs between cultures, within a being-not-one and as a being-not-one, relates to the universal repeated re-cognition which marks the reaching of its end point in the meta-context. It would still prove necessary to explain how, for instance, the 'contingent identity' of a German relates to the non-accidental rational identity of a citizen of the world, to which it is meant to direct all the other 'contingent identities', at least in Apel's view. If the unity of the meta-context remains untouched by the differences which mark particular contexts and distinguish them from each other, then these differences are not differences, they are simply moments of the unity which, as such, force the apologists of unification to explain the possibility of a division, a separation, a diremption without which the unity would not externalize itself and produce its finite moments. If, however, the differences which mark particular contexts, and distinguish them from each other, do affect the meta-contextual unity, then this unity is already something other than a unity, then the unification is itself not-one. To object to the notion of iterability for failing to take into account the 'potential for negation' which inheres in the 'validating basis' of acts 'oriented towards reaching understanding'; to believe that this failure is due to an erasure of those borderlines which legitimately separate contexts, which separate the 'problem solving capacities' of 'cultural systems of action' and the 'capacities for world-disclosure' specific to the 'art and literature business' (Habermas I, 205f.); to argue against the notion of iterability in the name of 'procedures' which are supposed to allow us to decide upon or to communicate about a meaning, an interpretation, the belonging of someone or something to someone or something (Menke II, 190); to reject the notion of iterability by pointing to the stability of a cultural 'background', of a virtuality which contributes to securing the meaning of communicating sentences, even if one must regard the 'background' as ultimately contingent, as virtual in the sense of its possible disappearance (Searle, 107) – always means that one dogmatically seeks to put an end to the transforming repetition and repeated transformation, or that one arbi-trarily and no less dogmatically cuts off the possibility of creating relatively stable contexts and 'backgrounds', from the possibility of radically destabilizing these contexts and 'back-grounds' – which amounts to an abstract separation of possibility and impossibility, to a purism of logical hierarchies, to a subjugation of the relationship between rule and exception to the rule, or to an exclusion by means of an inclusion. It is certainly possible to discern different 'forms of recognition' (Menke I, 94) in the movement of recognizing, to identify them in cultures and between cultures; but there is also a tension in the struggle for recognition which is triggered by the inseparability of all those particular forms from a deforming and disfiguring trait, from their transformability, from their sometimes unnoticeable and sometimes violent transformation into other forms with a differing or conflicting content. This inseparability affects and deforms the forms themselves, their being-a-form.

The universal thus reveals itself to be nothing but an unlimited series of generalizations, nothing but the invention of structures and rules which do not just serve the exchange of arguments in communities based on communication, nor the juridical and political organization of a society. Perhaps they fulfil the function of a journey through the emptiness of fields which extend into the infinite. We refer here to John Cage's concept of structure. During a journey through the emptiness of infinitely extending fields, an idea can come by at any time; at any time the forms of recognition can be suspended and deformed, given that we do not possess that which is repeated and that repetitions are perceptible or imperceptible changes. The universal proves to be a generalization or a universalization; the particular or the singular proves to be caught up in the aporia of that which cannot be repeated: without repeatability it would disappear, it would not appear as that which cannot be repeated. Its preserving repetition, however, delivers it to disappearance. This disappearance which cannot be opposed to the preservation of whatever disappears may be called cinders, a name Derrida uses for that which is im-pertinent, which does not belong, which does not remain and return, which is disseminated and lost. Cinders is a name for that which does not exist or which exists only without presence, it is a name for the cinders of cinders, for a burning which does not even leave cinders behind, for a passion of the absolute which is not the work and labour of the concept, which does not know of a determinate negation, a sublation, a transition or a passage through an endured death. Precisely because it thinks the possibility of a universal and a particular which are neither opposed to nor mediated by each other; precisely because it thinks an in-between without presupposition – the thought of recognition as a thought of iterability is neither a thought of the universal nor a thought of the particular, neither a meta-contextual thought nor a thought of single, independent contexts, neither a thought of an encompassing super-culture nor a thought of different cultures which exist for themselves. *As a thought and a praxis of iterability, the thought and the praxis of recognition are a thought and a praxis of an in-between without presupposition, of a middle which is not determined by fixed coordinates, of a medium which is not a supplementary element to be added to the elements which dwell within it and which it divides.* The way in which Derrida uses the adverb *quasi* indicates that iterability makes everything move away from itself, that nothing ever keeps to itself or remains what it is, not even iterability itself. Iterability cannot be a transcendental argument or law;

otherwise, the transgressive movement of repetition and change would be restricted and a meta-context would be established by introducing an untouched and untouchable conceptual ideality, an ideality meant to unify what is scattered and separated. We find iterability in Adorno's idea of a *musique informelle* which is not marked by an opposition between the compositional logic of twelve-tone music and free atonality: the compositional logic of twelve-tone music can no longer function as an 'inexorable tie'. We find iterability in the topological confusion, the quick traversal of juxtaposed rooms and spaces which are separated only by doors and yet do not communicate: the final frames of a film Hugo Santiago made in the second half of the seventies, *Écoute voir*, capture this topological confusion. We find iterability in Titina Maselli's figures which, painted on a surface without depth, traverse the urban landscape or are traversed by it. We find iterability in Sarah Schumann's pictorial strip which dislocates every phantasmagoria, every staging, every organization.

However, we should not overlook the fact that deconstruction experiences an interruption the very moment a quasi-conceptual argument shows that iterability must necessarily be included within iterability, and that recognition cannot but include itself within itself. What is at issue here is a transgression beyond the linguistic which does not lead to a meta-language, which lets itself be attracted by the non-deconstructible, by deconstruction *as* deconstruction, by deconstruction 'itself', by something which is neither an essence, nor a substance, nor a structure. What is at issue here is a transgression which becomes explicit at a certain point in time and which can therefore be interpreted as the instant of a certain exhaustion of deconstruction:

> That it [the concept of iterability] might belong to the class of concepts for which it must account *without* belonging to such

a class, that it might belong to the theoretical space it organ-
izes in a [. . .] 'quasi'-transcendental manner *without* belonging to such a space, is doubtless a proposition that can appear
paradoxical. (Derrida IIa, 127)

This passage makes clear that it is unavoidable to raise the following questions. How must we conceive of the interruption,
of the without of belonging, of the limit of deconstruction, of
iterability, of recognition, if we cannot conceive of it in terms of
a restitution or a presupposition of a conceptual and practical
ideality? What is it that shows itself on the limit touched by the
exhaustion of deconstruction? Does the thought of deconstruction
coincide with its exhaustion, or does such an assumption still
depend too heavily on an idealistic conception of history – on a
conception Derrida seems to hold on to, though perhaps ironically, when he considers the Aids epidemic to be a big screen on
which the virus of deconstruction somehow re-cognizes itself?

The limit of recognition is the divided line of an equivocation. It is not-one, given that it is both a link and an interruption, and that it brings together that which, as a limit, it separates.
The limit of recognition is an in-between which relates an immanence (between cultures) to a transcendence (the in-between
itself, the in-between as an in-between). Just as the impossibility
of determining criteria which allow for contexts to be kept separate unambiguously and for clearly assigning them communicated
messages, increases the responsibility for that which has been
communicated, rather than simply diminishing it; just as iterability
does not lessen the effort to determine what exactly has been
communicated and to do justice to the singularity of a communication; just as thinking and talking are torn between the
conditionality of contexts which can never be fully identified as
such, and the unconditionality of their openings which are never

pure openings or openings leading to something purely other; just as, torn between both, thinking and talking are restless and paralysed, exposed to the urgency of an impatient demand – recognition is embedded in an ongoing and endless struggle for recognition: the need, the neediness, the lack are always greater than the fulfilment, the realization, the achievement. Recognition produces a kind of bad or spurious infinity, it has the effect mythical violence has, if mythical violence manifests itself in the up and down of destruction and preservation. On the one hand, the insight into iterability makes the need for recognition even more pressing, not least because it itself can only be an insufficient insight, an insight which demands recognition. The need for recognition is never more unsatisfied than the moment the impossibility of its full satisfaction is re-cognized, or recognized. On the other hand, though, the recognition which, because of this particular recognition or insight, touches a limit, lets itself be affected by a letting-be. There is a letting-be of recognition. It can be understood in different ways. Recognition is a letting-be of the other, a breaking-off of a struggle, a provisional result of a process which lets the other be what he or she is, what recognition lets him or her be. But recognition is also a letting-be in another sense, in the sense of an interruption: one stops recognizing the other, one lets him be, because one does nothing but recognize the other, because one lets recognition be. *By recognizing the other, by remaining between cultures, in the in-between of cultures, one touches a limit of recognition; motivated and driven by the tensions in the struggle for recognition, one circulates between cultures, in the in-between of cultures, while at the same time entering the in-between itself, the in-between without presuppositions, the in-between as an in-between.* Because the letting-be designates the limit of recognition, because this limit, like every other limit, is an interrupted line, the interrupted line of an equivocation which

oscillates between recognition and something different from recognition, something to which recognition relates without relating to it, recognition lets itself be affected by a letting-be the very
instant it operates as recognition and touches a limit. Recognition becomes something different from itself, or rather, it becomes itself because it admits of a letting-be. One must not
confuse this admission, this letting-be with a submission, a retreat, a renunciation, for it occurs on a limit and as an experience of the limit. The letting-be can be found on both sides of
the limit or the border. It crosses it all the time, as it were. It is
traversed by the limit. One cannot determine or decide with
certainty which kind of letting-be we are dealing with. There is a
letting-be which is a stopping, a turning away, a suspending, a
letting go. To the extent that it occurs on a limit and opens up
the possibility of a beyond, it belongs to both sides of the limit
and cannot be clearly discerned as belonging to one side or the
other. There is also a *letting-be* which is a rendering possible,
a letting happen, an allowing for or an admitting of. Its effects
become evident on this side of the limit, in the struggle for
recognition; within this struggle, it allows for the movement
which seems to lead beyond the limit of recognition; beyond the
limit of recognition, it names recognition as recognition. There
is a *letting-be* which expresses the necessary equivocation that
makes it ultimately impossible to distinguish between the different ways in which it can be understood. *The letting-be is recognition (itself).*

Touching a limit, an extreme, the limit of recognition or its
exhaustion, means touching a being-not-one. If, for instance, the
Aids pandemic which has often been viewed as a wound inflicted
by an extreme development of Western societies, and as a paradigm of the social conditions of the West, is experienced from
an individual perspective as a destruction of a supposedly unified

and coherent life-context, a destruction caused by a premature death, then the only way of confronting this destruction is by measuring up to it and refusing to reintegrate the being-not-one into a consoling and reassuring being-one. What is at stake here is a being-not-at-one in recognition and as recognition, an impossible experience of that which proves to be resistant, of that which demands recognition and hence provokes resistance. To resist the resistance of the virus, it is necessary to proceed from an im-pertinent existence, from an existence which does not belong, from an originary being-not-one which can neither be a unity nor a simple origin, and which for this very reason is a limit concept. A limit links and interrupts, it cannot be identified, it cannot be comprehended by the unity of that which it divides and keeps apart. Therefore, to resist the resistance of the virus it is necessary to expose the being-not-one (of the limit, of existence) as such: this is the only way of being not-at-one with the being-not-one, of avoiding both, the apologetic negation of what is torn apart and its no less apologetic affirmation.

If multiculturalism is the result of an objectification and reification, it is most likely that the task of a multicultural politics or of a reactive politics of recognition will consist in securing the possibility of a more or less justified recognition between cultures; perhaps it will even consist in the creation of an encompassing super-culture which establishes a recognized ranking of cultures. The task of an active politics of recognition which does not objectify culture, which does not reify the act of recognizing and the in-between separating cultures and dividing culture, consists in bringing about conditions for an existence or a life capable of exposing the being-not-one of recognition as such: the being-not-one in recognition (between confirmation and establishment, homogeneity and heterogeneity), the being-not-one of the limit of recognition (between the perpetuated struggle for recognition and the in-between itself, its letting-be). The paradoxical import of this task, its immense and prohibitive difficulty become evident when one realizes that a being-not-one can never be simply exposed *as such*. For *as such*, it is already submitted to the unity (of a phenomenon) and deprived of that which makes it a being-not-one.

To exist under the conditions brought about by an active politics of recognition, is to exist without recognition, without justification, without grounding – without why. This is not because it stands in opposition to a why, a grounding, a just-ification, a recognition, or because it withdraws from them. In Heidegger's lecture course on the principle of reason [*Grund*] one encounters an enigmatically elliptical remark, an idea which is not developed in the context in which it occurs: for human beings to dwell in the 'most concealed grounds of their essence', they must 'in their own way' be like a rose – 'without why' (Heidegger II, 38). Within the immediate context of the lecture, this remark refers to a saying from Angelus Silesius. Hölderlin's verse about human beings as signs without interpretation, a verse Heidegger examines in a different context, resonates in this quotation. The fact that the distinction between different ways of being 'without why' marks a limit, an enabling limitation, or a number of enabling limitations, shows that Heidegger does not suggest that plants and humans should be regarded as equal. One has to distinguish between different ways of being 'without why' because the ground can have the character of a demand: where the principle of reason [*Grund*] reigns and where nothing is 'without why', humans are required to provide a ground. The ground is represented as a ground and each being as that which is grounded and stands on its own grounds. The period of time in which the principle of reason predominates is defined by Heidegger as the age of metaphysics. Metaphysics interprets the

Being of beings as a grounding ground which grounds itself, as ground of grounds. Since Heidegger tries to think the difference between Being and beings, and thus to think difference as difference, and since he has to explain how it is possible to interpret Being as a ground, he must on the one hand understand Being in terms of that which grounds, in terms of a 'letting-lie-present' which is an 'assembling' or a 'gathering', while on the other hand making clear that Being cannot ground and justify itself. If Being were to ground and justify itself, if Being as a ground grounding and justifying itself were a cause or a principle beyond which one cannot move, then it would once again be conflated with a being, given that only a being can be grounded and justified. It is by following this line of argumentation in his lecture course that Heidegger arrives at the point where he must formulate a strange sentence: '*Sein: der Ab-Grund*' ['Being: the abyss'] (Heidegger II, 111). Here, it is decisive that we do not give in to the temptation of a simplifying exegesis which places ground and abyss [*Ab-Grund*] in an oppositional relationship, reinscribing Being in the realm of representation. If Giorgio Agamben is right, if we can re-cognize Heidegger's thought by his use of hyphens, we must not dismiss the hyphen or the separation it marks in the abyss as an ornamental accessory or an archaizing alienation effect. Being is neither a ground nor an abyss, it presences as a ground and, as such, remains without a grounding justification, without a foundation. The limit of a separating and linking hyphen shows this presencing. It is not because Being withdraws like a being, for example like an absent God, that the presencing cannot be grounded and justified; it is because it presences as a ground.

Perhaps the formulation '*Sein: der Ab-Grund*' ['Being: the abyss'] which omits the copula and thus avoids defining Being and confusing it with a being, allows Heidegger to answer the question of a *regressus ad indefinitum* which, for thought, always presents a problem. Thought cannot but touch the limit of that which it thinks in order to think it in the first place – the very moment it thinks a thought, it cannot but exempt itself from that which it thinks. The thought of Being as thought of presencing or as thought of the abyss [*Ab-Grund*], the thought of iterability as thought of a belonging without belonging, the thought of recognition as thought of an in-between or of a letting-be, are each a thought of the limit. Because the limit is not-one, because it is itself a hyphen, one cannot simply cross it. The limit is an event, a happening which must be exposed as such; however, the exposure of the limit cannot presuppose another limit and therefore marks a limit of thought. The limit is an event, a happening to which one cannot relate from without, as one might to an object. If the thought of the limit as an exposure of its event or of its happening required another limit, it would not think the limit and its exposure would be forever deferred. In other words, *the thought of the limit encounters a limit and needs to become a praxis.* In the strange sentence, '*Sein: der Ab-Grund*', the first word is to be understood as a verb, not as a noun. The sentence has to be understood as an imperative: 'Be: the abyss'. If there is an exposure of the limit (of recognition), it can only consist in a transformation of existence into a limit. Existence then no longer recognizes something, it is itself transformed into recognition and exposes its letting-be, it exists 'without why'. It is from this perspective that Heidegger's enigmatic idea of human beings who 'in their own way' are like a rose – 'without why', can be deciphered. The 'most concealed grounds' of existence must be interpreted as the *Ab-Grund*, the abyss, and the task of thinking Being as Being can be carried out only by means of a transformation of existence, by means of a praxis. The '*entering*' or the '*retreat* [*Einkehr*] into the event'

101

Heidegger mentions in his seminar on 'Time and Being' has to be viewed as such a praxis. Derrida's demand for the invention of a political intervention which does not result from a calculation of the possible, but from an experience of the impossible, now appears in its radicality, too. The human who has become a hyphen and who thereby exposes the in-between, is without why. Without why is the human Adorno would have called emancipated: to describe him, he finds and repeats terms which express the absence of presuppositions Marx advocates when, in the *Eighteenth Brumaire*, he declares revolution to be a liberation from the presupposition of history and hence defines it as the end of tradition:

> Rien faire comme une bête, lying on water and looking peacefully at the sky, 'being, nothing else, without any further definition or fulfilment', might take the place of process, act, satisfaction. (Adorno IV, 157)

A reactive politics of recognition seeks grounds which can be recognized as presuppositions and preconditions necessary for the formation of a (cultural, ethnic, linguistic, sexual) identity. *An active politics of recognition looks for the possibilities of a transforming praxis which turns humans into beings without a presupposition.*

THE CULTURE OF POLEMIC

We're queer, we're here, so get fuckin' used to it

Someone wants to be recognized as a singular individual, as being this or that, because recognition promises an overcoming of the diremption and the dividedness of the one who is to be recognized, thus allowing him or her to merge into the unity of an identity and a coherent life. In her essay *The Agony of Europe*, published in 1945, María Zambrano writes that Europeans move constantly towards a projected ego while fleeing from another ego which leads a shadowy existence within them. She claims that it is possible to describe European history as the history of a heresy which leads to the birth of the European individual. An ego can be called European when it decides to exist and becomes independent from an already established order, separating itself from itself, splitting up into a double self. This ego is grounded in a flaw, in an absence, in a lack, which testifies to the violence of existence, of a decision to exist (Zambrano, 42). From the point of view of such an approach, not only confession, a concept discussed by Zambrano, but also recognition and the demand for recognition can be regarded as an historical attempt to overcome the diremption and dividedness effected by a being's decision to exist, by his resoluteness. The limit of recognition then coincides with the limit of decision-making and resoluteness, given that a resolute being which makes decisions always presupposes an ego which decides to exist and which constitutes itself through and within this founding act, this act of establishment and institution. There is a double limit here. On the one hand, there is the limit marked by the birth and death of the historical or European subject, a limit which separates it from a comprehensive (pre- or posthistorical) order. On the other hand, there is the limit marked by a transformation which must be distinguished from a 'successful' recognition, from a recognition by which the ego successfully overcomes its division into a given and a projected ego. All models of 'successful' recognition continue and extend the history of the deciding, projecting, recognizing, overcoming subject. In the context formed by such models, the limit of this subject is not thought and its transformation is not sought.

For this subject and for the theory of recognition that lets itself be guided by its concept, the question arises as to how one can re-cognize recognition, how one can grasp it cognitively. When can one say, when can one know, that an individual or a group has been recognized, that an individual or a group has not yet been recognized or is no longer being recognized? Is recognition bound to a shared experience, a regulated praxis, to gestural or specifically linguistic conventions and arrangements, to legal entitlements, to social and state-managed institutions? Or does recognition resist its re-cognizability, its cognitive identification; does it provide resistance against the subject and the theory of recognition which try to grasp it conceptually? Is the struggle for recognition always bound to a testimony which cannot be measured by unambiguous criteria? Take the slogan *We're queer, we're here, so get fuckin' used to it*, a slogan currently circulating in North America. As long as it retains its strike power and operates as a quick verbal attack; as long as it indicates a caesura which cannot be bridged by simply transferring and integrating this elliptical and yet utterly unequivocal phrase, intended as an offensive and polemical motto, into a legitimate, legitimated and legitimating discourse – the rhythmically repeated outcry testifies to a struggle for recognition. But the moment the slogan, the motto, the outcry, functions as a mere provocation which, like every provocation, feeds on an implicit agreement and a complicity with the provoked party; the moment the slogan is propagated by the bearers of a presupposed identity who profess to be such bearers, who as such bearers address themselves to bearers of a different identity in order to secure legal, social, institutional and political equality of status and treatment – the struggle for recognition disappears in a reformism which admits of differences only to the extent that they can be considered as valid differences, that is, as differences justified by their relation to a fundamental unity. The struggle for recognition disappears in the purist and puritanical uniformity of a 'political correctness' which proves to be the complement of misrecognition, exclusion and oppression. However, a reformism which in fact excludes the possibility of recognizing, must itself encounter the difficulty of achieving recognition of the fundamental unity of the grounds on which it stands. This unity does not have to be of a substantial nature, it does not have to depend on certain definite notions of content, it can result from the assumption and the acceptance of a formal equality in principle. Every reformism is caught up in a struggle for recognition, at least virtually; every reformism tries to regulate, delimit and direct the struggle, striving to turn its uncertainty into a certainty, aiming at security and stability. Reformism exposes itself to the struggle for recognition it attempts to comprehend and incorporate within itself. 'Wog, nigger, gook. Cocksucker. Use them right, the words have guts [. . .] Words such as faggot, wog, poofter, gay, Greek, Australian,

Croat are just excuses. Just stories, they mean shit. Words don't
stop the boredom' (Tsiolkas, 115 and 141).

We're queer, we're here, so get fuckin' used to it: who raises this
demand for familiarity? What is intended by it? If indeed there is
no unambiguous answer to both these questions; if only more or
less plausible, more or less probable answers can be given; if the
plausibility or probability of such answers is dependent upon a
contextual insertion and determination for which there can be
no ultimate criterion – then the dispersal or the dissemination of
the demand can be understood as an effect of iterability. Its
interpretation itself requires an act of recognizing. To interpret is
to recognize. But it is precisely this need for a recognizing interpretation and for an interpreting recognition; it is precisely the
dispersal and dissemination of the demand; it is precisely the
iterability – which allows the demand to be raised as a demand.
One could never raise the demand *We're queer, we're here, so get
fuckin' used to it*, one could never interpret this slogan as a
demand, as the interconnection of an assertion and a demand,
if it were possible to determine its meaning and its function
unambiguously, if it were possible to prove conclusively that it
is nothing but a demand, a pure demand. For a demand without
uncertainty remains inconceivable, as has been shown. *We're queer,
we're here, so get fuckin' used to it* – if this phrase, this motto, this
slogan is to be understood as a demand for recognition, then,
like all demands for recognition, for confirmation and establishment, it appears to be riven by a contradiction and held in
suspension by an ironic trait: one is asked to recognize that
which no longer needs to be recognized. We who demand
recognition are already what we are, not at some other place to
which you have no access or which you can avoid; this is precisely why we demand recognition in your very midst. Only if
you, to whom our demand is addressed, get used to what you

must get used to and to what in a certain sense you have already got used to, only then are we what and where we are, in the midst of you. The necessary contradiction inherent in the demand for recognition allows for the following translation of the slogan: we who raise our voice in our own name because this name and this voice are not yet our own and because we must appropriate them, are here without being here; we are what we are without yet being what we are – for this reason we demand that you recognize us and get used to the fact that we are here as what we are. Only when you get used to our being here and to our being what we are; only when you thereby recognize us, even though you do not need to recognize us, given that we are already here, in your very midst – only then will we be able to say that we are here and that we are what we are, that we have a name and a voice. The demand for recognition is a demand for confirmation and establishment, yet the slogan connects and separates assertion and demand in the paradoxical blind spot of a 'so', in the simultaneity of a continuity and a caesura, of a conclusion and an opening. It can be noted in principle that the contradiction, the irony, the diachrony in this simultaneity impedes, indeed robs the speakers and agents of all possibilities of easily contrasting their own *we* with the *we* of others, or of drawing a clear distinction between those who demand recognition and those from whom recognition is demanded, between those who make the demand and those to whom it is addressed, those from whom something is demanded. The *skandalon* of the slogan, the irreconcilable polemic of the phrase, its illegitimacy before any possible legitimacy and legitimation, resides in the equivocation it brings about by conflating the *we* of those to whom a demand is addressed and the *we* of those who address the demand – a *we* which seems to stand out and to set itself off more strongly than ever, for it is the *we* of those who throw the slogan at the others like an arrow which has already hit home when its whistling flight alerts the victim to the imminent danger. It is a repeatedly re-cognizable slogan and a barely intelligible outcry, an impertinent suspicion and an act of violence beyond all argumentation, a declaration of love and a declaration of war, an exclamation whose sharp contours and whose wounding sting allow no undecided, hesitating, sentimental foe to measure himself against it; it is an exclamation whose measure can be taken only by the foe Jean Genet sought in an imaginary newspaper advertisement: 'blind, deaf and dumb' because he is given no room to manoeuvre, no room for negotiations, a foe 'without arms, without legs, without belly, without heart, without sex, without head' (Genet, 9). On the one hand, there is scarcely a doubt as to who the demanding subject is and what the demand is about. On the other hand, however, the boundaries between the subjects, who are not as yet subjects, remain permeable. The demand cannot be immediately and repeatedly re-cognized as being this or that demand.

The boundaries remain permeable, the borders are insecure and the frontiers open; this openness, this insecurity, this permeability is also caused by the possibility of interpreting the word *fuckin'* as the object of the familiarity the slogan wants to establish ('get used to'). Once again, those who propagate the slogan appear to be the ones who recognize, while those to whom it is addressed and who are receivers appear to be the ones who demand to be recognized and who struggle for recognition. From the viewpoint of such an interpretation, the ones who are struck by the slogan must themselves struggle in order to obtain and deserve the recognition of those who recognize only reluctantly and, for this very reason, are recognized as bestowers of recognition. Bestowers of recognition who are not, in Michael Walzer's words, 'reluctant givers' (Walzer II, 254), bestowers of recognition whose generosity does not reside in their hesitation, their restraint, their aversion, in a sense of responsibility, are in greater need of recognition than the ones who demand to be recognized. The open economy of recognition contains a non-democratic trait, a one-sided dependence which makes it unsuitable for producing the closed economy of a reciprocal repeated re-cognition in which the dependence could be overcome. This does not necessarily mean that recognition exercises a disintegrative effect, quite the contrary: to the extent that the act of recognizing never reaches a conclusion; to the extent that it is always put off balance and held in tension by a one-sided dependence, by an asymmetry and a relationship between heterogeneous forces – it seems to encourage that decisionistic moment of stoppage which produces an irresistible integrative effect, an effect which crystallizes in the collective gathering around whatever has been arbitrarily recognized. A thinking and a politics of recognition that underestimate or fail to recognize the danger of such decisionism, precisely because they conflate the act of recognizing with a repeated re-cognition, will always remain powerless against it.

The insuperable difficulties with which the slogan *We're queer, we're here, so get fuckin' used to it* confronts the theory and the subject of recognition are particularly noticeable when this phrase, this outcry, this motto, functions as a privileged example of all possible demands for recognition. It explicitly strives to secure the maintenance of an established relationship of recognition through habituation and habit. A demand for recognition cannot simply be a demand for the establishment of a recognizing relationship resulting from a struggle for recognition, a struggle the demanded establishment brings to a conclusion; it must always also be a demand for the maintenance of the established relationship, it must demand fulfilment and continued fulfilment, since a fulfilment without a long-lasting effect, a fulfilment which is not a continued fulfilment, proves to be nothing but a postponement or a deferral of the demand. In other words, the habituation which makes the establishment of a recognizing relationship possible while being kept in suspense by something unusual and unaccustomed, by the unfamiliarity which allows an act of recognition to be such an act in the first place, must be transformed into a habit, at least if the demand for recognition is to be fulfilled truly and effectively. No subject of recognition would be a stable and reliable subject if habituation did not result in habit – if the ones who recognize did not get permanently used to the ones who are to be recognized, if the ones who are to be recognized did not get permanently used to the ones who recognize. The fatal character of this necessity lies in the fact that habit threatens the repeated re-cognition of recognition which is fundamental to the continuation and the maintenance of a relationship based on an act of recognition. Does habituation not consume the act of recognition which depends on it? Is it not the case that an indifference which discriminates against that which is different tends to assume the form of a habit, as does a domination which conceals itself? Are those who have been recognized not rendered invisible by habit, does habit not erase their difference? Is there a more effective means to fight recognition than habituation, a habituation without which recognition would not come into existence? Habit is the monument and the ruin of recognition. It is always possible to denounce the theory, the historical and conceptual investigation of recognition, the investigation which traces the history of the concept and which must exempt itself from the struggle for recognition, as a form of oppression, as a suppression, an extinction, a perversion of that which is to be recognized, as an unacceptable, ideological, power-driven subsuming of the act of recognizing under an excluding repeated re-cognition, even if such a theoretical investigation justifies its exemption or its exceptional status on the grounds that it alone allows it to do justice to the act of recognizing.

The slogan *We're queer, we're here, so get fuckin' used to it* is a speech act which cannot be controlled by any subject, an outcry one appropriates only to expose it to another virtual or actual appropriation, to a different interpretation or recognition. This exposure takes place at the very moment the outcry is appropriated, domesticated and classified. *We're queer, we're here, so get fuckin' used to it* is indeed a queer slogan, an orphan which always behaves differently to what the family expects, a displaced and displacing partisan whose fighting behaviour is irregular, whose increased mobility puts him beyond the pale and whose tactical agility destabilizes the 'tellurian' character and the defensive posture of the 'classical partisan' (Schmitt, passim). *Because recognizing is both a confirmation and an establishment, every demand for recognition behaves like this outcry or like this slogan; every attempt to think recognition results in a queer thinking or in a thinking of the queer.* Whoever demands recognition has already arrived at his destination, is already where he still has to get to; he does not require the recognition he demands. His polemical presumptuousness consists in the fact that he, the one who wishes to be recognized, transforms the others, the ones who are meant to recognize him, into those who have to be recognized. Thus the roles, functions and positions become involved in an uninterrupted and uncontrollable exchange. Ultimately one cannot decide who it is that is supposed to be recognized here and now, and who it is that is recognizing the other here and now.

The pressure on the here and now is increased all the more by the fact that there is no horizon from which one could recognize the permanent switching of positions, functions and roles as an aberrant or deviant exchange and hence turn it into

111

a regular and regulated circulation. Therefore recognition, which duplicates every integrative effect by means of a disintegrative one without ever allowing for a positive dialectic to recuperate integration and disintegration and to assign them a meaningful, fixed determination, proves unsuitable for an all-encompassing identification that might ensure an enduring stability. Yet recognition is indispensable if one is to identify with a group, a people, a country, a state, a tradition, if one is to identify these entities as such and to re-cognize them, if one is to re-cognize oneself in them and to do so repeatedly, if one is to be re-cognized by them. For identifications must transgress a boundary and thus require an act of recognition in order to clear the way for the repeated re-cognition at which they aim. Attempts to justify nationalism, for instance, are thwarted by recognition, even if their object is the enlightened 'nationalism of the present', the 'nationalism of this day' that Oriol Pi de Cabanyes, director of the Institució de les Lletres Catalanes, tries to infer from the 'interrupted identity' of a people. Instead of placing the 'Catalan tradition' in opposition to other traditions, instead of anchoring the sense of national belonging in the 'closely-woven fabric of the past' or deriving it from a 'planning of the future', Pi de Cabanyes turns to the present. The here and now of a Catalan 'version' of what is supposed to be universally human should form the basis for a nationalism appropriate to the times (Pi de Cabanyes, 88f.). The notion of such a 'nationalism of the present' results from the fear of violent nationalistic excess and extremism, of 'unhealthy forms of nostalgia' and 'futuristic fanaticism'. Yet the idea of an ahistorical, purely isolated here and now which refers to a transhistorical, entirely abstract essence of humanity without really accounting for the nature of the relationship between the universality of this essence and the particularity of its versions or manifestations, is unconvincing. The 'nationalism of the present' remains a nationalism, and for this reason proves to be excessive: it contains the extremism it is meant to exclude. The symptoms of a contamination become apparent when Pi de Cabanyes speaks of those interferences and interruptions which are 'undesirable' and which the 'nationalism of the present' is meant to keep away from the 'interrupted identity' of the Catalan people.

The identity of the Catalan people is an interrupted one. Like all other identities, it cannot insulate itself from the intrusion of an alien externality. If it could, it would immediately fossilize. Pi de Cabanyes distinguishes heritage, experience and interruption in order to emphasize the violence and the inevitability of the interference, of the interrupting intervention. If it is true that the identity of a people is an essentially interrupted identity and thus non-identical or at odds with itself, then a people can never have recourse to the organic totality of a past or to the seamless appropriation of a future. The justification of the interrupted identity of a people must lead to the conception of a 'nationalism of the present'. To the extent that such a justification is linked to a nationalistic conception, it tends towards extremism and excess, towards an exclusionary appropriation of a totality, towards the demarcation of a boundary that circumscribes a permanent state of belonging in which interruptions are subjected to control and the feeling of difference serves an unimpeded self-assertion. The interrupted identity, the identity which is inscribed in the movement of recognition and thwarted by it, turns in the end into a unified identity, into the identity of an identifiable, repeatedly re-cognizable subject which repeatedly re-cognizes (itself). The plan, the projection, the program of a new nationalism is the ideological conception of a unification without interruption, of a will to unalloyed self-presence which puts past and future at the disposal of such a presence:

The full responsibility for what we will become at any time in the future will be ours even more clearly. Our own temporal existence will be even more stable and balanced because we will have a precise knowledge and an appropriate consciousness of the fact that we have been Catalans for a thousand years, that we are what we are and that we will be what we want to be. This balance will probably be our strongest defence against all presumptuous interferences, against all undesirable interruptions and interventions. (ibid., 91)

If the one who recognizes the other is at the same time someone who is recognized, and if the one who is recognized is also someone who recognizes the other; if the here and now of recognition is a then and there – why not interpret the splitting of recognition into a confirmation and an establishment, a splitting which supposedly brings about and prolongs the struggle for recognition, the bridge-burning polemic, the partisanship of displacement, as the balance and the harmony of a reconciliation? Can confirmation and establishment not be seen as being complementary to one another? Why insist on a vertiginous, uncontrollable, disconcerting exchange of positions, on a general de-positing? Because confirmation and establishment are heterogeneous acts and because the heterogeneity marked by their difference can be overcome only by the dogmatic presupposition or the postulation of a repeatedly re-cognizable unity, of a unified repeated re-cognition; it can be overcome only by the elimination of recognition itself. The slogan *We're queer, we're here, so get fuckin' used to it* is a caesura loaded with tension, an interruption which cannot be bridged, an invasive, irruptive, surprising presumption, a queer and unruly, expropriating and dispossessing outcry which eludes and resists all appropriations.

Consequently, it would be a trivialization, a euphemistic interpretation to reduce this slogan to a demand for a reassuring habituation, for a concurring readiness to put up with something, for an understanding endurance and a reasonable toleration of those nameless individuals intended by the pronoun *we*. Though one cannot and should not exclude an interpretation of the slogan that views it as a demand for the 'transformation and reformation of socially valid regulations', for the acceptance of the in-difference which characterizes the recognition of the nameless and which alone can do justice to difference in a society (Menke II, 77f.), one must equally keep in mind that something about the slogan remains intolerable, unreasonable and insulting, something connected with its exclamatory nature. For the slogan resists both the ideological preformation of the legal system which disadvantages those who raise the demand and the anonymity of the societal context regulated by legal norms; it resists the equanimity or 'in-difference' of the regulations, whether they be 'formal' or 'effective' in kind. Such an 'in-difference' is either a selective one, in which case the condition of its possibility consists in the by no means 'in-different' decision as to who is intended and implied by it (soundness of mind of those it intends and implies, responsibility for one's actions, etc.), or it is an undifferentiated 'in-difference' which intends and implies everyone, so that no real recognition eventuates at all. In truth, this is because of the necessary and constitutive mechanism of selection it requires. The 'in-difference' of the nameless proves to be a virtual normality, a normality which saves itself up and which consolidates its forces, a normality which has already withdrawn from its excluding, minimizing and marginalizing manifestations the instant one tries to call it by its proper name. As is the case in Andrew Sullivan's apologetic pamphlet *Virtually Normal*, the difference of those who have been recognized, in

115

which virtuality concentrates and accumulates, marks nothing but a distance which enables normality to affirm itself ever more forcefully and relentlessly.

Of course, one need not pay the price of a naive intentionalism or contextualism if one distinguishes a 'political recognition' from another kind of recognizing, and uses this distinction to indicate the difference between the sphere of namelessness and the sphere of names. But one does revert to a naive intentionalism or contextualism if one asserts that the name of the political is reserved for the namelessness of the social context presupposed by the 'non-political' or 'sub-political' spheres of recognition. For the political dimension and the politics of recognition require the opening which suspends recognition; the challenge of the unpredictable slogan *We're queer, we're here, so get fuckin' used to it* bears witness to the effects of this opening. It is precisely this opening which makes politics necessary. Must not the political ensuring and securing of the leeway we allegedly require in order to experience whatever solidifies in 'non-social', 'sub-social', 'non-political' or 'sub-political' forms of recognition (ibid., 94), be constantly exposed to insecurity and suspension if the 'in-difference' towards difference is not ultimately to lead to assimilation, to a levelling-down of differences, to the namelessness of erased names? The moment one can clearly discern and delimit the framework within which differences may occur, the moment it has been established that a framework encompassing all differences does exist, the moment it has been decided in advance that only 'relationships involving adult love and friendship' (ibid., 92) characterize a certain 'non-social', 'sub-social', 'non-political' or 'sub-political' domain of recognition, to give but one example, the slogan *We're queer, we're here, so get fuckin' used to it* has been emptied of everything that can account for its political virulence, because difference has already been domesticated and robbed of that which makes a difference. The slogan is an unbridgeable caesura not only in a juridical or legal domain which must be transformed, but in all domains where recognition proves to be determining and decisive. This is not to deny that the irreducible tension which traverses recognition is a tension which exists between asymmetry and symmetry, and that the demand for the creation of secured political domains is inscribed in the struggle for recognition just as much as is the destabilizing disjunction of the securing delimitation of a domain and the leeway which transgresses limits. Politics is the name for the carrying-out of the conflict looming in this tension, between name and namelessness.

Asymmetry and symmetry, confirmation and establishment are not invariant forms of a concept. They are stabilized elements of a recognition different from repeated re-cognition, of a recognition which has to be distinguished from a re-cognition and which is marked by a tension: if this tension is dissolved, if it disappears in an achieved and successful recognition, then the distinction and the difference between the act of recognizing and a repeated re-cognition are eliminated. The modes and ways of recognition, its times and its opportunities all result from the *constellations* and the *configurations* of its elements, and cannot be classified according to a stable hierarchical relationship, a stable relationship of precedence and derivation, of presupposition and dependence. The act of recognizing subverts such relationships wherever they have solidified, wherever they have become independent of it. Surely there is a difference between talking about the recognition of a people struggling for political autonomy, and talking about recognition in love and friendship; at the same time, however, the various forms of recognition and their respective configurations are subject to a deformation, are part of a movement which cannot be grasped with concepts

117

of form or formlessness. As soon as the act of recognizing is conceived of in terms of a reformism which relates it to the presupposed unity of a general 'in-difference' or to an achieved recognition, to a recognition which is regarded as a result, it is misrecognized. Recognizing is misrecognized as soon as one believes that one can actually re-cognize it, re-cognize it repeatedly, and measure misrecognition by the criteria or the standards of such (repeated) re-cognition.

The misrecognition of recognition which inheres in its reformist concept, *and which could not even be conceived of without its continuous destabilization*, has one important consequence. To distinguish minorities and majorities that struggle for recognition may well serve as a reformist strategy within the horizon formed by the unity that a formal equality establishes, but it also afflicts the struggling majorities and minorities with a dangerous blindness. Whoever distinguishes majorities from minorities and subscribes to this majority or to that minority, can only confront the incommensurability and the measurelessness which the movement of recognition entails by attempting to reduce that which stubbornly resists all measurability, transforming it into something measurable and measured, something commensurable with quantifying and identifying factors. In an essay on the question of measure and the issue of how majorities and minorities are constituted, such as it is discussed in the debate concerning multicultural societies, Werner Hamacher writes:

> For a claim which is incommensurable with a merely quantitative representation based on equivalences, a voice must make itself heard precisely within this representation – another voice and perhaps something other than a voice. The commensurable must make itself incommensurable, the countable uncountable. (Hamacher, 313)

Minorities that fight for recognition and majorities that recognize them are blind to the anarcho-revolutionary violence of the measureless, of that which is without measure, of that which is not of the nature of measure. To put it differently, a group which identifies itself as a minority can, fundamentally, no longer struggle for recognition and has already lost this struggle by virtue of its own impotence. When, on the street of some North American city, someone shouts 'Hey, faggot!', the recognized individual, the individual who relies on an achieved recognition, feels outraged. But the individual who makes no claim to an achieved recognition simply invents a different war machine.

The suspicion that no one is more powerless and impotent than the person who has struggled for recognition as the member of a majority or minority, adducing more or less convincing reasons and encountering more or less success; that, despite appearances, the recognized individual proves to be the most impotent and helpless, not only because of a possible revocation of his or her recognition, but above all because of his or her relative inviolability – leads to the realization that recognizing, an act, a process, a movement which does not solidify, which opposes reification and which never becomes re-cognizable as a recognition, thwarts the possibility of the *as*, of recognizing something *as* (being this or that). A moment of balance, of equality, of homogeneity, is indispensable to the act of recognizing, to the struggle for recognition, and keeps promising such a possibility; it even opens it up. Yet it also suspends it, given that it cannot be isolated or determined as the result of a dialectic. In the struggle for recognition, the pre-predicative or linguistically articulate *as* which determines something in its specific quiddity, is separated from itself before it can form a unity, before it can affirm itself as the *as* itself, as the *as* of an originary or a modified understanding. If one follows a suggestion from Michael Walzer, it is sensible to distinguish an explicit and complex recognizing *as...* from a 'simple recognition' (Walzer II, 258), from the general expectation with which a member of a society might reasonably approach another. However, all recognizing which serves to ensure a balance, to secure an order, to stabilize a framework, and which is supposed to satisfy general expectations, is implicitly a recognizing *as...*, a recognizing whereby the one who is recognized becomes repeatedly re-cognizable as a member of a group. Such a group is delimited by a framework and held in balance by an existing order. *Thus the struggle for recognition reveals itself to be a struggle for the as, for the structure of the as-such; it reveals itself to be a struggle for the possibility of revealing-oneself-as-something.* The reification of the act of recognizing which extinguishes it and comprehends recognizing only as the repetition and confirmation of a presupposed given, *as* a recognizing *as...*, should consequently not be confused with the act of recognizing and the struggle for recognition. In the end, recognition *as...* proves to have concealed or excluded the alterity of the process of recognition. The consequence of this concealment or this exclusion is that one does no longer recognize, and that one is no longer recognized, precisely because one only ever recognizes oneself. The struggle for recognition turns into a struggle of the subject which attempts either to include otherness within itself, or else to exclude it from itself. The politics of recognition becomes a fundamentalist and immanentist politics, regardless of the intentions and instruments with which it operates. We can discern here another limit of recognition, a limit drawn by the annihilation of otherness effected by an absolute re-cognition, by a repeated re-cognition which constitutes the aim of 'my struggle' – of *mein Kampf.*

BETWEEN CULTURES

Aids

The fact that one is recognized *as* this or that, that one recognizes this or that *as* something, that one recognizes this or that *as* this or that, means in terms of the contemporary politics of recognition that one repeatedly re-cognizes that which is to be recognized and the ways and modes of recognizing. The question of the singularity and the cultural specificity of a form of life which is often raised in order to object to abstraction in general and above all to philosophical abstraction, is based on such a misrecognition of recognition, on a confusion of the act of recognizing with an act of identification. One wants to know what it really means to lead an existence *as* X; one is mistrustful of and hostile to the universalization effected by philosophical abstraction. The phrase 'you *as* X' ascribes a particular knowledge or attributes a singular experience to a distinctive and incomparable position, to a position both impregnable and untenable. Having become independent of all content, it functions as a signal to be re-cognized and belongs to the jargon of multiculturalism and difference which has inherited the legacy of affliction and affection left by the jargon of authenticity. One is no longer affected and afflicted by an existential limit-experience which leads to an overcoming of the singularity of a specific existence and transforms the one who makes it into a singular and special individual; one is now affected and afflicted by the mere experience of existence itself. This experience is already a limit-experience given that existence is supposed to consist of nothing but its corresponding singularity, of nothing but the diversity of identities which demand to be recognized as such. The demanded confirmation of a recognition *as...* is the instrument with which one tries to do justice to a singularity and to resist its dissolution into a discriminatory generality or universality whose difference tolerates no other difference.

In debates revolving around the constitution and nature of multicultural societies, nations and states, the experience of a singularity is often interpreted as a linguistic experience. Having analysed Catalan language and reduced it to its most simple component parts, one can claim to find within it the irreducible specificity of that which is Catalan, the 'identifying trait or feature' of its identity – such is the proposition put forward by Pi de Cabanyes (Pi de Cabanyes, 95 and 124). The trait or feature which is meant to mark a historical *differentia specifica* of the human race, contains the possibility of a recognition *as...* and of the identification with other peoples whose identity has likewise been suppressed on the grounds of their difference. Pi de Cabanyes wishes to uncover an affinity between the internal and external experience of exile made by Jews and Catalans. The usage of one's own language thus becomes a tool by means of which one opposes the suppression of one's singular identity, of an identity defined by its elementary linguistic peculiarities. How do the singular and the universal relate to each other between cultures? This question proves to be a question of *language and its usage*. Along with Wittgenstein, Adorno is one of the philosophers who, in the present age, have strongly emphasized the significance of the usage of language. The transforming adoption of the motif of a language of names did not weaken his intellectual sensitivity to the dependence of whatever is being said on the usage made of language; on the contrary: it rather strengthened it. This sensitivity demonstrates its worth in Adorno's analysis of the jargon of authenticity and of a 'teutonizing cabbalism', as well as in his remarks on the function of foreign words and punctuation marks. If the usage and that which is being used coincide in the language of names, then finite languages are traversed by the tension which exists between both and which inaugurates the history of language. The temptation for a language which is being used to manifest its independence from any particular usage is inscribed in this tension; a purely self-referential usage must remain a pure possibility and reinforce the usurped independence of a language. When the words which are being used become autonomous and virtually independent of their usage, language falls prey to a mystification which surrounds it with the aura of the numinous, or it begins to function as the carrier of discri-minatory prejudices. Jargon, the usage of what cannot really be used, betrays the profane basis of such a mystification. The abrupt breakthrough of violence resulting from the thoughtlessness with which one uses this or that word indicates and denounces the prejudice in the chatter which reveals the becoming autonomous of usage. Such chatter can be interrupted and resumed at will, given that it seems to be independent of the speaker and the spoken. It ultimately makes no difference whether language becomes autonomous and independent of its usage, or whether it is usage that becomes autonomous and independent of the language used. In her literary work, Nathalie Sarraute has given expression to linguistic movements in which language and its usage become autonomous and independent of each other:

He didn't do it on purpose, of course he didn't, what do you think, this word merely escaped him, it is only padding, a connecting word he sometimes happens to use, unintentionally, without trying to puff himself up, without pointing his finger at something and reducing it to ridiculous proportions . . . just look at him . . . he would be amazed by all this agitation, all those border crossing troops, all these constricting threads, all that linguistic artillery, all the tow-lines, the foreign languages, the frogs, the oxen, all the scalding vapours, the bubbles, the games, the contortions, all the tremulous attempts . . . what an oversensitive nature, what a vindictive, suspicious, arrogant mind . . . and really, wouldn't he be right? How could we live if we were to take umbrage at the slightest little thing, if we did not very reasonably just let pass such words which after all are quite insignificant and innocuous, if we were to make such a fuss about so little, about less than nothing, for nothing at all? (Sarraute, 108)

Thus the identifying recognition *as...* does not serve a free usage of the self's own, but *an own usage of the self's own*. It lets language slip into jargon or chatter. But both jargon and chatter escape the act of recognizing.

If one thinks and acts on the grounds of such a scheme; if one transforms recognition into a means of identification which is supposed to allow the identified difference to affirm itself – then it proves to be quite consistent with one's assumptions to insist vehemently on the specificity of experiences. The specificity of experiences made by people with Aids would be one example here. The virus circulates between cultures without a cultural specificity, a singular tradition, a particular identification or allegiance limiting the danger of an infection and preventing the continuation of the guerilla war to which Luc Montagnier compares the attack on the immune system. Recognizing is as resistant to re-cognition and repeated re-cognition as the virus itself; a re-cognition and a repeated re-cognition which result from a misrecognition of the act of recognizing and which serve the purpose of an immunization against the dispersing effects of its resistance, try to break the resistance of the virus by identifying its carriers. Thus the usage of a philosophical terminology in a discussion about Aids is sometimes sufficient to give rise to the suspicion that the activity of the virus which weakens the immune system is being redoubled. If the specificity of the virus consists in the dissolution of all the specificities which are meant to ensure the possibility of an unambiguous identification of its carriers, then one suspects any theory which abstracts from specificities of inflicting on the carriers what the infection has already inflicted upon them. One suspects theory of extinguishing its very object.

Of course, the argument linked to such a suspicion is not always a summarily developed argument directed against theory as such. In his conceptually confused treatise on an indispensable and inalienable 'gay specificity', a work which is also to be read as a 'celebration' of universality, as a 'celebration' of the 'homoness' in 'all of us', Leo Bersani leaves no doubt as to the pertinence of an analogy which relates the consequences of Aids to a paradoxical struggle for recognition. This struggle for recognition is paradoxical because it increases and simultaneously reduces the visibility of those who are to be recognized. To criticize the idea of a recognition *as...* and of a specific identity which is to make possible a repeated re-cognition, is considered to be a threatening move, a kind of identification with the aggressor which triggers the coining of a neologism in response. According to Bersani, the gay man's struggle for recognition, so critical of the idea of a specific identity, proves to be a 'de-gaying'. The strategy of the argument, the equating of the one to be recognized with the bearer of an identity whose irreducible specificity is to be re-cognized repeatedly if it is to resist the universal, the world as it is, is not immediately affected by the question of the way in which such a specific and resistant identity is to be grasped and comprehended – does it make sense, for instance, to speak of the 'indeterminate' and 'mobile' identity of a universal and yet particular homo-ness? In Bersani's eyes, the increased visibility of gay men produced by Aids is to be understood as the monstrous promise of an invisibility brought about by death; therefore, the theoretical endeavour that dissolves specificities and identities, creating the ubiquity of a ghostly universality, operates like the present and yet absent virus:

> Invisibly visible, unlocatably everywhere: if the gay presence is threatened by absence, it is not only because of the secret (or not so secret) intentions of those who are fascinated by gays, or even as a result of the devastating work of Aids, but also because gays have been de-gaying themselves in the very process of making themselves visible. (Bersani, 32)

When it is a politics of identity, a politics which takes recognition to be both a presupposition and a result, the politics of recognition splits up into two extreme positions. Its proponents either cling to an identity whose specificity or singularity cannot be dissolved into a generality or universality, or they attempt to relate a particular and singular identity to a universality and to mediate the former with the latter. In the latter case, the particular and singular identity is granted its right to exist only by virtue of its relation to the universal with which it is mediated, whilst in the first case the affirmation of its singularity depends precisely on the resistance to the universal, on the impossibility of a mediation and communication. If it is true that the suspicion of universality, to which a politics of recognition gives rise and which clearly comes to the fore in the debates centring around the Aids epidemic, is nourished by the insight or the supposition that the mediation of the singular and the particular with the general and the universal only conceals the extinction and eradication of the singular and the predominance of the universal, then the identifying recognition of the singularity of a virus carrier and the insistence on the difference which marks the experiences made by infected individuals and people with Aids – a difference which sets these experiences apart from the experiences of other individuals – have a threefold function. The recognition is intended to resist the levelling caused by the virus and thus the virus itself; it is intended to destroy the ideology according to which only certain groups can be affected by the virus; finally, it is intended to counter the 'monopolization' of the infection by particular groups.

Thus to the extent that Aids stands for a threat provoked by a dissolving universality, one can maintain that one of the most influential versions of the politics of recognition effects a polarization of the universal and the particular. This polarization pushes both terms to a limit at which the particular is directly exposed to the universal. At this point, recognition is supposed to strengthen the immunity of the particular and also to guarantee it. One must ask oneself whether such a polarization does not in fact perpetuate a bad infinity, an endless conflict which tears the two poles apart from each other. That the politics of recognition keeps splitting into two contradictory and irreconcilable tendencies which cling either to the irreducibility of the particular or to the primacy of the universal, seems to confirm the assumption that it remains caught up in a bad infinity. Attempts to mediate are doomed to failure, since it belongs to the notion of a successful mediation to sublate the particular and to bring it back to the universal. Without such a sublation the mediation remains incomplete and the tension between the universal and the particular is perpetuated. The universal is disavowed by every particular instance which is not brought back to it and thereby sublated, by every singularity which escapes universalization. Conversely, every singularity which can be brought back to the universal without leaving a remainder, every singularity which in the end does let itself be subordinated to the universal, is not a singularity, but only a finite figure of the universal. Even Bersani's teetering between an assertion of the specific and its universalization, even the ambiguity which renders the assertion and affirmation of the specific dependent on its generalization, shows that a politics of recognition cannot solve the problem whose solution would alone legitimate it, and that it cannot do so as long as it continues to be guided by the traditional opposition between the universal and the particular, privileging the one or, alternatively, the other. To object that the universal which is postulated or presupposed by the universalistic version of a politics of recognition should not be conflated with the ideological construction denounced by the defenders of the particularistic version, prolongs the bad infinity just as much as transforming the particular and the singular into an absolute which takes itself to be the only measure. However, the realization that the struggle for recognition is triggered by the act of recognizing and that the act of recognizing can never adopt the form of a result, of a recognition which has been achieved successfully, without being misrecognized and confused with a repeated re-cognition, need not also and necessarily lead to the affirmation of a bad infinity. For the question raised by such a recognizing realization, by such an insight into recognition, is the question of how to relate to the blind spot, to the trace of the split which separates the act of recognizing from

128

itself. One constantly encounters the blind spot of recognition, despite the impossibility of ever identifying it; one comes across it again and again precisely because of this impossibility. Since recognition is a recognition only to the extent that it splits up into a confirmation and an establishment, into a relationship of homogeneity and heterogeneity; since a blind spot makes the insight into recognition itself a recognizing insight; since recognition moves between the universalization and the singularity of its reiterations – the question a thought of recognition must ask is neither the question of a universality which can embrace the particular nor the question of a singularity which manages to maintain itself unchanged, affirming its authenticity in the face of the universal. *It is rather the question of the ways in which thought and the blind spot, the being-not-one, the in-between of recognition, are to be related.*

Consequently, thinking and talking about the Aids epidemic does not mean that one refrains from all talking and all thinking whose object is not an invoked and evoked singularity, unmistakable and incomparable. It means that one relates to the in-between of recognition, an in-between one cannot attribute to the universal or the particular, an in-between which is not the middle and the medium in which a mediation occurs. The politics of recognition cannot be located in the particular or the universal; it cannot protect the particular from the universal or bring back the particular to the universal. A singularity which relentlessly resists universality by virtue of its excluding and exclusive character, and a universality which regards the particular merely as its alienated figure, cannot be recognized. It is impossible to relate to them, given that they are absolutely re-cognizable, that they can be repeatedly and absolutely re-cognized, and that for this very reason they elude any attempt at relating to them. But if the universal and the particular cannot simply be mediated with each other and if they cannot be isolated from each other either, if this is why they require a recognizing behaviour, if thought has to relate to the in-between, to the in-between of the universal and the particular as the in-between of recognition itself, then thought finds itself in a vicious circle. It must recognize the in-between of recognition and also relate to the in-between of this recognition. The necessity of relating to the in-between of recognition must therefore be understood as a task: as the task of opening up the circle, as the task of a transforming praxis by means of which thought transforms itself into the in-between to which it relates. Such a transformation would amount to thought ceasing to be a recognition, a relating to or a behaviour.

In order to illustrate the necessity of opening up the circle of recognition, a necessity which reveals itself to be a task, one can refer to selected passages from the novel *Le fil* (*The Thread*), written by Christophe Bourdin from the perspective of a person with Aids, and to a paragraph from Adorno's 'Meditations on Metaphysics' which deals with the history of death, with its historical and societal mediation and inscription.

1. Does death make us mortal? Does it turn us into finite beings? Not quite, it seems:

> The fact that I must die of Aids, that from the point of view of statistics all people with Aids have died, is a knowledge which to this day and in my own eyes has not made me entirely mortal. (Bourdin, 138)

If death does not make us entirely mortal and if our knowledge of death does not coincide with what we know about ourselves, then we are perhaps always already mourning death. We mourn death because we let it die again and again, or because we again and again bring death to it. Without this peculiar reflection of death and mourning, without this mourning which mourns death and mourning, we could not relate to death at all. If death were an absolute event, an abstract boundary, it would be impossible to recognize that we are mortal, finite beings. As finite beings we relate to death, to our own death and to the death of the other; yet by relating to death, we already survive ourselves, we become immortal before we can even ask ourselves how we relate to death. Death makes us immortal. Of course, the survival which crosses the border of death, which transgresses its boundary, is not only a mourning which, in mourning mourning, puts an end to mourning. It is still a mourning, a mourning in the course of mourning mourning. There is no survival which does not survive the self: when we survive and when we thus survive ourselves, we become other, we become a witness who attends the process of dying and mourns the one who is dying. The survivor is a witness; he can find himself in the position of a mother who remembers her son in the presence of a young man with Aids. This man, her son, has aged prematurely; for him, nothing happens at the right time any more: 'Perhaps she also tried to remember the one whose loss she was now attending; perhaps she tried to see me as the son whom she was remembering in my presence' (ibid., 106).

The other, the witness of my dying whose memory mourns for me, the other as witness of myself, the other in me is a double other. He is a mourning other who still belongs to the living. His memory tries to restitute my life, to give it back to me. At the same time, however, he also belongs to the dead, to the deceased who survive their death: 'The others, the deceased, those who are already dead, can lead me to myself better than anybody else' (ibid., 135). Let us put forward the following hypothesis: Death, which we name and to which we thereby relate, names the death of death; its naming anticipation mourns mourning.

But the immortality of the mortal is never able to extinguish death. As an interrupting and incommensurable event, as an event which marks the impossibility of all possible events and which for this very reason cannot even be called an event, death is not something to which we can relate. We cannot deal with death or behave in accordance with it. The mourning which arises from the impossibility of a relationship to death, from the preceding forgetting, from the originary amnesia which resides in such an impossibility, proves once again to be a mourning which mourns mourning, a mourning which mourns the impossible relationship to the impossible. Let us therefore put forward a second hypothesis: Finitude splits into two extremes and is the name of a double mourning which each time mourns mourning; it names the fact that we relate to death and yet cannot relate to it.

How are we to think the possibility of mourning if we take into account the impossibility indicated by the double mourning which each time mourns mourning? Perhaps this possibility can only be thought by being attentive to an in-between: mourning takes place between one death of death and another death of death, between one mourning which mourns mourning and another mourning which mourns mourning. The death of death is never simply a death of death, the mourning which mourns mourning is never simply a mourning which mourns mourning. Let us put forward a third hypothesis: What is called finitude refers to the separation and the relation of an in-between which maintains death and mourning in an irreducible tension.

The hypotheses we have put forward so far lead to conflicting conclusions which cannot be reconciled. If death and mourning are not terms identical with themselves, it seems to be inconceivable that we ever die at the right time, at the time when it finally becomes possible 'to unravel the thread of the days which keep accumulating' (ibid., 89), the 'invisible thread which connects everything a single person has amassed during his whole life, no matter how difficult it is to connect the things amassed' (ibid., 152). Can death – which is not death and which therefore does not occur or come at the right time – transfigure the causes and the symptoms which have robbed the mortally ill patient from those 'imaginary vertical threads' (ibid., 76) which hold the healthy individual upright? Can it imbue these causes and symptoms with a meaning? If we lived and died at the right time, we could not mourn: the possibility of mourning depends on a radical contingency which transforms death into a death before the time, into a premature death, into a death which comes too early or too late, which occurs and does not occur because it is not identical with itself. However, mourning would be just as impossible if we could not relate to death at all, if we remained simply exposed to a radical contingency. The non-identity of death and mourning thwarts the immediacy of such an exposure, while still exposing us to the radical contingency of death. Let us put forward a further hypothesis: Finite beings die neither before their time nor at the right time.

The Aids epidemic appears to give greater visibility to the non-identity of death, to the division of finitude into conflicting and coinciding extremes. On the one hand, one cannot relate to death if one can no longer abandon oneself, if one is ill and nailed to one's own sick body (ibid., 104–5): this captivity is a crucifixion without resurrection, an endless self-reference resulting from the impossible relationship to one's own death. It finally deprives the one who is ill from any possibility of relating to something, to himself or to another person. On the other hand, one still relates to death: the one who is ill tries to survive death by incorporating and thus forgetting the virus which circulates in his blood. This peculiar coincidence of memory and forgetting within an appropriating incorporation or assimilation promises the fulfilment of a twofold demand and once again leads to the impossibility of relating to something. The pure survivor who extinguishes death by completely appropriating it no longer relates to himself or to another. Survival plays an incredible trick on finitude:

> How can I manage to reconcile two contradictory demands, the demand to forget myself and the demand to remember myself, the demand to assimilate my illness and the demand to conjure away the most important event of my life? (ibid., 143)

The fact that death is not identical with itself means that there is a history of death, a history which is constitutive of death, not one which would remain external to it or leave its supposedly invariant essence untouched. It means that, on the one hand, all statements about death can be dismissed on the grounds of being mere generalizations or hypostasizations of a specific historical determination, and that, on the other hand, all attempts at determining the historical changes death undergoes can never be content with the specificity of a single historical determination. The increased visibility the Aids epidemic gives to this non-identity, heightens the tension between universality and particularity, for one is torn between generalizations which ascribe to the epidemic an enlightening, displaying, revealing character, and the recognition of the singular, i.e. the insistence on the different ways in which the appearance and spread of the virus have affected certain groups while sparing others. One teeters between the abstraction of theory and the critical exposition of the specific reasons for inequalities; one teeters between a decontextualizing conclusion and the concrete effects inequalities have on groups affected and on their struggle for recognition; one teeters between the transcending philosopheme and the intransigent analysis which resists generalizations, the analysis of the social, political, historical, economical, medical, institutional, geographical, demographical conditions which have allowed the epidemic to take hold.

2. In Adorno's 'Meditations on Metaphysics', one passage reads as follows:

> The statement that death is always the same is as abstract as it is untrue. The manner in which consciousness comes to terms with death varies along with the concrete conditions under which people die; this varying extends into the physical. In the camps death has a novel horror: since Auschwitz, fearing death means fearing worse than death. (Adorno I, 464)

These unequivocal sentences which emphasize the historical mediation of death and which are probably directed against Heidegger, precede another sentence which must surprise the reader, precisely because it links directly to the argument developed so far while taking it in the opposite direction:

> What death does to the socially condemned can be anticipated biologically by observing loved ones of a very old age; their body, their ego, everything that determined them as human beings crumbles without an illness or a violent act intervening. (ibid.)

Renouncing all mediating arguments, Adorno goes from the most extreme concretion which Auschwitz drastically calls by its name, to the abstraction of a general or universal biological condition which is illustrated by an example. From the horror of the camps and the death of those who are 'socially condemned', he switches directly to the death of 'loved ones of a very old age' without the line of argumentation being explicitly affected or altered by this sudden change. The use of the verb 'anticipate' even allows us to conclude that the irreducible singularity and specificity of any possible relationship to death and of any possible consciousness of death have always already been superseded and recaptured by the universality of a biological condition. The argument is covertly reversed, as it were. Of course, Adorno's postulation that historical and social mediation extend into the physical, places the discussion of a universal biological condition once again in the light of a particularity which limits the claim to universality. No matter how plausible such an interpretation proves to be, it must be stated that the logic of the argument presented in the above passage contains a blind spot. If one reads the passage from the point of view of the argument, the mediation of the universal and the particular is not achieved, without the lack of mediation being itself justified. It is as if the mobility of thought opposed the age of dogma. The reader must therefore ask himself how he is to relate to this blind spot, to the unmediated leap in a line of argumentation which on the surface and at first glance remains undisturbed. He must ask himself what it means that only a recognition can relate to such a blind spot, a recognition which should not be confused with a mere coming-to-terms, given that it reproduces within itself the blind spot through which the one who recognizes becomes caught up in a kind of bad infinity, in a bad infinity for which every access to a positive infinity is forever blocked. The passage in question is the cause of a constant irritation, since it cannot be interpreted, or rather, since it forces the reader to abandon himself to the infinity of contradictory interpretations which again and again reveal themselves to be unsatisfactory and which for this very reason keep referring to each other, as if the passion of the possible were ultimately to dissolve all actuality and all reality.

136

THE CULTURE OF CRITICISM

Recognition as presupposition and result

The concept of recognition is mostly used in the contexts of social philosophy and philosophy of right, at least in current debates. It is possible to use it in these contexts because the struggle for recognition always indicates what in traditional terms can be called an exiting from the natural condition or from the natural order of things. Social philosophers raise the question of a politics of recognition in debates about the organization of multicultural societies; they ask what the implications of such politics are and what they should be. Particularly in the United States, culture is not just understood as the culture of peoples or ethnic groups. Minorities in general interpret their identity as a cultural one. To speak of 'gay roots', for instance, seems to make sense only if a link between minority, identity and culture is presupposed. Identity is to be recognized and is to take root more securely through its recognition because it appears to be already rooted in the ground or in the soil of culture, and because its identical, unified and repeatedly re-cognizable roots already secure the homogeneity of culture and of cultures. Difference and singularity are thus reified. Alain Badiou apodictically states that no specific and concrete situation can ever be clarified by an ethics of culturalism which appeals to the 'recognition of the other' (Badiou, 27). Perhaps Badiou's statement can be taken to mean that nothing is more indifferent than an objectified difference and a reified singularity, even if he defines difference in general as that which simply exists and which is 'deposited' by truth in its very happening.

Yet precisely because a politics of identity comprehends culture as something homogeneous, as a multiplicity of homo-geneous cultures whose repeated re-cognizability guarantees the homogeneity of the totality, of a totality which also vouches for each culture, it is unclear how far the roots extend and how deep they reach. An ambiguity appears at this point. On the one hand, the roots are meant to anchor the distinctive particularity of an identity; on the other hand, they are meant to allow for a generalization of the particular, for a perceptive and intransigent tracing of neglected, tell-tale details in the culture of the other. 'Gay roots' and a repeatedly re-cognizing recognition belong together:

> 'No homosexuality in Kubrick's work? How about two very buffed men with lots of spare time only nominally guiding a space ship through space? What about a very fey HAL killing and disposing of his rival, and his last pathetic attempts to curry favor with his beloved singing 'Daisy, Daisy, give me your answer do' (Davey, Davey)? It's one of the most beauti-ful if tragic love stories on film. Methinks you need to see it once more.' David Lippe, San Francisco. Arts editor Chris Culwell responds: 'If *2001* is one of the most beautiful tragic gay love stories on film, then what are *My Own Private Idaho*, *Mala Noche*, *The Living End*, *The Boys in the Band* and all those other films that concern themselves directly – not through innuendo – with the love between homosexuals? *2001* is not a film about homosexual love, and if you think it is, methinks

you need to see it again, along with the aforementioned flicks.'
(*Bay Area Reporter*, vol. 24, no. 31, 4 August 1994, 7)

The fact that the debates which deal with the organization of
multicultural societies tend to circle around the interpretation of
the multiplicity of identities and cultures, rather than addressing
the concept of culture itself and that which makes a different
culture into a culture in the first place; the fact that the discontent in culture is normally not interpreted as a discontentment
with culture denotes a prejudice, a preliminary judgement, a
preliminary decision, a recognition before all recognition which
unifies the manifold and misrecognizes the act of recognizing.
But conceptual naivety avenges itself, not because the conceptually naive is not capable of using a reflective and appropriate
concept of culture, but because the lack of conceptual reflection
prevents one from touching the limits of a concept of culture,
i.e. its constitutive and ultimately inconceivable being-not-one.
The prejudice, the preliminary judgement or decision which
informs recognition, leads to culture's functioning as a unity
which holds together the manifold and the unified elements of
unification. The movement of recognition which is neither a
purely natural nor a simply cultural movement, but a transition
to culture, is subordinated to a recognition *as...*, to a reification
and objectification which contains within itself the primacy of
culture. A struggle for recognition which has not been manipu-
lated by such a reification and objectification takes place in a
culture or in a multiculture; however, it also puts culture itself at
risk. If recognition is split by a 'structural unconscious', then it
can be said that the act of recognizing creates a discontentment
in and with a (unifying) culture; this culture constitutes itself in
a struggle for recognition, in a struggle whose possibility must be
sought in the struggle between the life and death drives, between

Eros and Thanatos, at least from a psychoanalytical point of view. To the extent that culture keeps reproducing a discontentment within and with itself, a discontentment which is not simply cultural, recognition *as...* suppresses culture; it suppresses the culture to which it refers when attempting to establish a cultural identity and to secure the rootedness of identity in culture.

The 'politics of recognition' which today has become a predominant ideology, is characterized by a largely dogmatic belief in a culture whose correlative is a politically, historically and philosophically no less questionable celebration of the irrationally natural. But what other fundamental traits or characteristics mark this ideology? One can try to discern such characteristics by privileging more or less well known, more or less influential, more or less symptomatic texts written by more or less recognized social philosophers or theoreticians. Their coherence and their consistency seem to be determined by a misrecognition of recognition and by the hypostasization of recognition *as...* Two fundamental characteristics of the prevailing 'politics of recognition' which are inseparable from each other and from the dogma of culture can be found in texts whose authors are Jürgen Habermas, Axel Honneth and Charles Taylor.

First characteristic: recognition as presupposition and result

Whenever recognition is defined in terms of something that has been achieved, as the end of a struggle in which single individuals or a group of individuals struggle for their identity; whenever the essential indeterminacy of recognition is traced back to a determination or to determinacy; whenever the moment of homogeneity, of balance, of symmetry is considered to be more than a moment exposed to heterogeneity, imbalance and asymmetry; whenever this moment becomes independent and is extrapolated from the struggle for recognition on the grounds of the dependence of a struggle on a preceding and completely indeterminate recognition of the other; whenever it determines the concept of recognition and provides it with its conceptual unity – recognition proves to be both something which is already presupposed and secured in its being presupposed, and something which is already a result and secured in its being a result. The politics of recognition one can adhere to under the sign of such a philosopheme of unity and unification, is located within a closed horizon in which the other cannot be recognized, but only repeatedly re-cognized *as* this or that other, *as* the bearer of this or that identity. Recognition *as...* makes difference disappear the very moment the recognized individual affirms his or her difference and thus asserts himself or herself. However, the emergence of a result which transcends the struggle for recognition is not its last phase, just as the preceding recognition is not its first, initial phase, a phase which comes before the struggle for recognition and which renders it possible. If there is a moment when a completely indeterminate and pre-thematic recognition transforms the other, and if there is a moment when recognition seems to solidify into a result, then these two moments must be considered to be traversed by a tension and therefore to be split; one moment is *already* split, the other one is *still* split.

The unifying strategy of a politics of recognition which is a politics of recognition *as...* or of repeated re-cognition, becomes apparent in Charles Taylor's lecture 'The Politics of Recognition', first published in 1992. In a passage where the willingness to be open to comparative cultural study entails a recognition of the possibility of transforming one's own cultural understanding and hence an opening of the horizon within which members of a particular culture understand something (Taylor, 73), the openness to other cultures is said to be meaningful only on the basis of a hermeneutic-methodological condition. For it to be meaningful, it must refer to an always possible and necessary 'fusion of horizons' (ibid., 67). Although Taylor announces that he wants to take a step back in order to understand how the discourse of recognition and identity became a familiar discourse, he does not analyse the 'logical' implications of the concept of recognition. He leaves it at an historical overview which hardly considers the logic of the concept, a logic that Hegel for example develops in his exposition of the dialectical constitution of self-consciousness.

At the end of his lecture, Taylor concedes that the horizon of *all* horizons, the horizon which comprehends *all* horizons within itself and which cannot be fused with an additional horizon because all horizons have already been fused together and have formed this 'ultimate' horizon, is a distant horizon, a horizon barely visible on the horizon. In other words, one cannot as yet re-cognize the value of particular cultures whose horizons are to fuse together in a teleologically determined process of understanding; the creation of a *truly* multicultural society, of a society in which the particularities of particular cultures have merged into a super-culture which integrates their divergence, remains a present and future task. Must not the 'ultimate horizon', if it is to be such a horizon and not just a border to other worlds with other horizons, be unrecognizable and indiscernible, at least to some extent? Must it not remain at an immeasurable distance which constitutes its transcendence and which cannot be diminished by coming closer to it? Must it not permanently defer the ultimate insight into the value of cultures? The transition of recognition into a repeated re-cognition – which all recognition anticipates – is located by Taylor in the vague future of a super-cultural creation or establishment. But Taylor has no doubts as to the necessity for a politics of recognition to let itself be directed by an (ideal) super-culture which by virtue of its global format is and must be the result of a selective process of unification. In Taylor's eyes, not *all* cultures, cultural forms or sub-cultures have 'something important to say to *all* human beings' (ibid., 66 – emphasis A.G.D.). A heliotropism of history is at work in such an approach. If an '*ultimate* horizon' can be said to exist *realiter* or *idealiter*, then a politics of recognition cannot but turn to it and must have recognized the possibility of a horizon of all horizons. Under such circumstances, recognition is always already a secured result, it is always already secured in its very presupposition, regardless of the historical adversities, the lack of respect and the humiliation to which those who struggle for recognition are exposed. But does a struggle for recognition take place at all if it is surrounded by an 'ultimate horizon', if the horizon is an ultimate and therefore a primary horizon?

Taylor is forced by his own approach to conceive of the fusion of horizons, a fusion which creates an 'ultimate horizon', as a process of selection, as a series of decisions about exclusions, at least if he wants to bestow a determining and determinable meaning upon recognition. Yet the final fusion can never fully succeed, given that the ultimate and inescapable, beyond which one cannot move, exposes itself to that which it has excluded, to a spectral return which perpetuates the struggle for recognition to infinity. The fact that the exclusions are meant to be based on an actual or ideal unanimity, not on arbitrary decisions and actions, does not really make a difference. Not even the approval of the ones who have been excluded or who decide to exclude themselves after an act of successful self-criticism would suffice to gain control over the effects of the exclusions, for an exclusion is defined by its withdrawal from the self-consciousness of the ones who are excluded and of the ones who exclude. An exclusion effected with the full and undiminished awareness of the excluding subject and the subject excluded, a self-exclusion as act of an entirely autonomous subject or of an intersubjectivity entirely in control of itself, of an intersubjectivity inheriting the legacy of a God separating himself from himself, would not amount to an exclusion. It would be nothing but the wilful, arbitrary self-limitation of an abstract unity, of the abstract One which cannot make the experience of the other and which revokes its self-limitation before it can even limit itself.

The determination of the 'true locus' of hermeneutic philosophy remains strangely out of focus, presenting itself as the determination of an 'in-between' which Gadamer describes as an 'in-between' of 'strangeness and familiarity', or as an 'in-between' that separates a 'historically intended, distanciated objectivity' from a 'belonging to a tradition' (Gadamer I, 295). Both the horizon of understanding and the fusion of horizons which occurs in the eventful 'process of transmission', a process that mediates between past and present and hence is a constant understanding mediation, are affected by the blur in the topology of the hermeneutical truth. In contrast with this blurred picture, Taylor's projection of a completed 'process of transmission' which is surrounded by an 'ultimate' horizon, a projection oriented towards the future which has come to terms with the past, seems to provide a much clearer picture – the picture of an objectification whose immutability, in fact, strikes one blind. Taylor renounces the possibility of thinking an in-between and an eventful process; he renounces the possibility of thinking the in-between of recognition and recognition as an event, as a happening. But what causes the blurring and the indeterminacy which splits the determination of the 'true locus' of philosophical hermeneutics and produces an in-between of the in-between, between the in-between of the eventful process and an objectified in-between, an in-between without event? The blurring and the indeterminacy are caused by the fact that a hermeneutic understanding recognizes the otherness of a text which needs to be understood; that it thwarts the enlightening insight which 'denies tradition its power' and recognizes 'that all understanding essentially involves some prejudice' (ibid., 270) which enables and marks it; that it preserves the eventful 'process of transmission' in the affinity with or the 'assimilation of tradition', presupposing a radical notion of history, a historicity which, in principle, makes it impossible to resolve the historical tension into a 'knowledge of oneself' (ibid., 302); that it postulates the mobility of its own horizon and therefore conceives of the fusion of horizons as an open-ended process – while *at the same time* outlining the 'meaning of the whole' (ibid., 267), of the whole of a text and of the whole of the tradition which requires understanding: it hypostasizes this meaning by assigning the historical mobility of a horizon to its own circumference and placing the in-between of strangeness and familiarity in the circumscription of an all-embracing, surrounding 'single horizon' (ibid., 304). Yet in view of such a reintegration, the act of understanding which belongs to the continuous 'process of transmission' is always also a 'standing within' [*Darinstehen*] tradition (ibid., 282) which must be understood as a well-grounded stance and an interruption of the eventful process. Some kind of interruption is no doubt necessary if one wishes to understand and thematize the eventful process in which one partakes; however, it submits the being-not-one of the process to a being-one which is indispensable for fusing horizons 'in a regulated way' (ibid., 307).

What does Taylor's super-cultural or uni-multicultural idea of a politics of recognition have in common with the approach we find in Habermas and Honneth? Habermas and Honneth recognize difference only under the aspect of universalism because they want to avoid particularism and fundamentalism; their approach is similar to Taylor's in that it fails to recognize the indeterminacy essential to recognition. This misrecognition of recognition effects a conceptual simplification with far-reaching political consequences. It somehow programs the arguments of the three social philosophers. Prior to any consideration of content; prior to any decision on the 'ethical content of a political integration encompassing all citizens in equal measure'; prior to any decision on the relevance of 'differences which, within a state, exist between various ethical and cultural communities, between communities which refer to respectively different conceptions of the good in order to secure the integrative force of their cohesion' (Habermas II, 144) – the conceptual simplification, which is a truncating reduction of the act of recognizing, subordinates the politics of recognition the three social philosophers try to justify, to the political instances which unify, normalize and discipline: the state, the institutions, the police.

Honneth's project is based on an identification of the 'basic motifs of a morality of recognition' and aims at reconstructing a social struggle for recognition. Thus it is inseparable from a politics of recognition. On the level of political and societal organization, the 'moral competence or accountability' this social philosopher speaks of repeatedly in his inaugural lecture when describing the 'idealizing anticipation of conditions for a successful and undistorted recognition' (Honneth I, 260), must be safeguarded by instances which ensure that 'moral irresponsibility' does not distort recognition after all. Such instances must look after those to whom 'moral competence or accountability' cannot be attributed (as yet or any more). Even an interpretation of the struggle for recognition which would be capable of showing that it denotes the 'results' of an irreversible 'moral progress' (ibid.) and that the 'conditions for a successful and undistorted recognition' can ultimately be posited as absolute or unconditional conditions, as conditions under which all thinking and acting individuals are capable of forever preserving their 'competence' or 'accountability' – even such an interpretation would have to exclude retrospectively the individuals deemed 'morally irresponsible', the individuals who did not survive the struggle for recognition untouched. This exclusion would be immediately and automatically justified by the fact that it would have proved possible to create integral 'conditions for successful and undistorted recognition'. It would, however, expose the 'morally competent or accountable' subjects to being haunted by the 'morally irresponsible' ones. The 'morally competent or accountable' individuals would once again have to establish instances which would protect them against the dangers of an irresponsible behaviour; they would have to attempt cognitively and affectively to appropriate any previous maltreatment without ever being able to transform the past event into something which never happened, and without ever being able to exclude the past exclusion. Their 'moral competence or accountability' would invariably perpetuate and prolong the possibility of an irresponsible behaviour.

What programmed stages of argumentation are repeated in the arguments that Habermas, Honneth and Taylor present? In each case, the first stage of argumentation leads to emphasizing the relevance of recognition for the formation of individual and collective identities. In each case, the second stage of argumentation leads to dissolving the act of recognizing into an achieved recognition, and thus to reducing it to a relationship of integral reciprocity. In each case, the third stage of argumentation leads to attributing to the struggle for recognition the function of a double integration, and to privileging this function over other functions: recognition is said to constitute the identity of an individual or of a group, and thereby to (re)generate the presupposed identity of the whole or of the totality.

Only if one is willing to follow these stages of argumentation, recognizing them on the grounds of their persuasiveness, can one, as Habermas does, let oneself be guided by the premise that a basically continuous and always preserved link exists between a universally binding legal system and those (cultural) differences which can be distinctive of particular social groups. From this point of view, the external (the political reality of a state and of its constitution) and the internal (the reflected self-understanding of an individual or of a group) cannot diverge historically in such a way that they become antagonistic forces. The 'unrestrained revisionism' Habermas supports, a revisionism which can even effect a 'breaking with one's own traditions' (Habermas II, 142), and the 'unshackling of communicative liberties' (ibid., 145) which contain an 'anarchic core' (Habermas III, xi), are both essentially limited because they are not supposed to affect the positing of a unified 'universe of discourse' (Habermas II, 144) and of a 'common horizon of interpretation'. The argumentative logic of the discourse cannot unfold if such a universe and such an horizon are not presupposed. Thus the 'structure of the conditions of mutual or reciprocal recognition' remains 'intact' only to the extent that a recognition before all recognition, a recognition which is legitimated by the logic of the discourse and which recognizes a presupposed or previously posited unity, allows all subjects subsequently to 'look at things from the other side's point of view' (ibid., 149) and to derive their strength from that 'power to transform oneself' (ibid., 143) which turns cultural disintegration into an integrating 'interaction with those who are foreign and with that which is alien' (ibid.). It remains unclear, though, how the 'self-transformation' can be reconciled with the 'split identity' which, according to Habermas, sometimes separates self-consciousness from itself in multicultural societies, pointing beyond a 'conscious break with tradition' (ibid.). How deep into the unconscious can the split actually stretch if a 'split identity' is still to be revived by the 'power to transform oneself' without which cultures are unable to stay alive and 'legal guarantees' lose the grounds on which they can be given?

The presupposition of a unity demanded by the logic of the discourse is not a cognitive achievement. As a positing, there is always something blind and mythical about it, something forced and imposed upon the individual. If, on the one hand, the positing inscribed in a logic of discourse requires to be recognized in the name of rationality, then, on the other hand, the being-not-one of recognition also dis-places the positing, diverting it from its course. The question which arises at this point, the question of the relationship between rationality and recognition, cannot be asked by discourse ethics. For the reification or objectification of the struggle for recognition, its transformation into a result, finally transforms recognition into a repeated re-cognition and knows of recognition only as a virtual repeated re-cognition. Freedom is unleashed, liberty is unshackled because it has previously been tied back to the economy of the whole, i.e. because the movement of recognition has been confiscated, as it were, in order to renew incessantly the integrative force needed to hold together multicultural societies and to secure their democratic constitution. One cannot but conclude that a politics of recognition which owes its existence to such a confiscation must surrender itself to an unpredictable and uncontrollable dynamics of integration and disintegration whose (often violent) consequences it then has to endure.

The tension which marks recognition and which also causes it to appear as a movement (between the one-sided, the asymmetrical, the unbalanced, the unequal, the heterogeneous *and* the reciprocal, the symmetrical, the balanced, the equal, the homogeneous) can never be completely dissolved. Therefore, the confiscation of the movement of recognition leaves traces, as can be gauged from the following example. On the one hand, Habermas maintains that the 'right to democratic self-determination definitely includes the right of the citizens to insist on the inclusive character of their own political culture', since this culture protects society 'against the danger of segmentation' (Habermas II, 147). On the other hand, however, he writes that 'political integration' does not legitimate a 'compulsory assimilation in favour of the self-affirmation of the cultural form of life prevalent in a particular country' (ibid.) – an assertion which is separated from the one quoted previously by only one single sentence. The subtle distinction between an 'insistence' which, if it is really to be an insistence, ultimately cannot tolerate any compromise, and a 'compelling' which remains incompatible with recognition, is a highly precarious distinction. It is a distinction or a difference whose unstable form points to a conflict Habermas does not re(-)cognize: to the conflict inherent in the act of recognizing.

Second characteristic: idealization as ideologization

The movement of recognition is charged with tension; it is contradictory, divided and distorting. An idealization and an 'idealizing anticipation' become an ideologization of recognition the instant they bring its movement to a standstill, as if it were possible to exit from the struggle for recognition, at least *idealiter*, because it itself tends towards the ideal or the idea one associates with recognition, with the notion of a 'complete' and 'successful', 'intact' and 'untouched' recognition freed of all tensions and contradictions, of a recognition which has come to terms with itself and which has come into its own, of a recognition which finally exhibits its true, repeatedly re-cognizable, 'undistorted' form or figure.

What precisely is meant by the overarching and anticipatory orientation without which Taylor, Habermas and Honneth cannot conceive of recognition? What is meant by an orientation towards an 'ultimate horizon' (Taylor) that recognition strives for, by an orientation towards a projected 'association of free and equal individuals' (Habermas) that points the struggle for recognition in the right direction, by an orientation towards 'conditions for a successful and undistorted recognition' (Honneth)? To the extent that it is indebted to the logic of discourse, the project of an 'association of free and equal individuals' remains dependent on a 'transcending anticipation' which is implied in the 'recognition of normative claims to validity' (Habermas III, 21). A consensual theory of truth which is appropriate to the logic of discourse cannot avoid referring to a concept of recognition. Thus if it is not to remain essentially 'in need of clarification', it must confront the difficulties the formation of a concept encounters in the movement of recognition at the very point where it is a matter of comprehending recognition and grasping it conceptually. Is the recognition which establishes the rational consensus a mere repeated re-cognition which removes or sublates all differences? Can a recognition provide the struggle for recognition with a direction and an aim? How do the 'conditions for a successful and undistorted recognition' relate to the struggle which they provide with a direction and an aim? *Either* such conditions can be brought about *in the real world*, in which case one must not only explain why they have not been brought about so far, but also ask whether the fact that they have failed to come into existence in the past does not expose them to a contingency which will always distort recognition and prevent it from succeeding. *Or else* bringing about these conditions and a successful recognition is an ideal, an idea which informs the struggle for recognition without ever reaching an end *in the real world*, in which case one must raise the question of whether it is not the irreducible ideality of the idea that prevents recognition from being a recognition. According to Adorno's insight, 'utopia is blocked off by possibility, never by immediate reality' (Adorno I, 57). This is the paradox of the idea: the closer one gets to it, the more it appears to turn away and the more distant the 'conditions for a successful and undistorted recognition' seem to be. The one who approaches an idea does not say 'The more you ignore me, the closer I get', but rather 'The closer I get, the more you ignore me' – or, to be even more precise, he says 'The closer I get, the more you ignore me; ergo, the more you ignore me, the closer I get', and so on.

Since Taylor, Habermas and Honneth do not follow up the implications of these questions in the account they give of a politics of recognition, they pave the way for an idealization which functions as an ideologization. The effects of an idealizing ideologization are particularly noticeable in Honneth's inaugural lecture. Undeterred and with undiminished self-confidence, Honneth speaks of a 'free control over the body', of the 'ability to coordinate autonomously one's own body', of 'fully adequate and morally equal partners' who, when interacting with each other under conditions of a 'successful and undistorted recognition', guarantee 'constant reassurance'. It remains entirely unclear how reality and ideality relate to each other in this account of a recognition which succeeds in being what it is meant to be.

One would like to find out, though one does not, how Honneth interprets the idea of an 'autonomous control over one's own body', of a control which must be recognized as a primordial and indispensable condition for the succeeding of an undistorted recognition, in debates triggered by the questions of incurable diseases, suicide and abortion. Ronald Dworkin, for instance, writes in his book *Life's Dominion*:

> Justice Scalia [. . .] was even more explicit in stating that the intrinsic value of human life does not depend on any assumption about a patient's rights or interests. States have the power, he said, to prevent the suicide of competent people who rightly think they would be better off dead, a power that plainly is not derived from any concern about their rights and interests. If such people's taking their own lives is wrong, this is in spite of, not because of, their rights. It is because their lives have intrinsic value – are sacred – even if it is not in their *own* interests to continue living. (Dworkin, 12)

And:

> I shall also try to show how judging life in that way presupposes an even more basic premise: that we are ethically responsible for making something worthwhile of our lives, and that this responsibility stems from the same, even more fundamental idea that I argued is at the root of the abortion controversy as well, the idea that each separate human life has an intrinsic, inviolable value. (ibid., 27)

One would like to find out, though one does not, how Honneth interprets the pre-established harmony between body and soul, a harmony he must postulate at least with negative formulations if recognition is to succeed and appear undistorted and unfalsified, in debates triggered by the questions of psychophysiology, psychopathology and psychoanalysis. The 'preventive treatment of illnesses' is harmoniously linked to 'the social guarantee of relations of recognition which are capable of providing the subject with the greatest possible protection from an experience of disrespect' (Honneth I, 252). If 'psychological "health"' amounts to the preservation of the 'integrity of the human being' and if it results from a 'successful and undistorted recognition', then it depends on this harmonious link, on this correspondence, on the symmetry, the balance, the simultaneity which characterizes the relationship between body and soul, or between body and mind. In this model the harmony is and must be pre-established, for otherwise the 'social guarantee' would not be permanent; its permanent ratification would be fundamentally called into question.

One would like to find out, though one does not, how Honneth interprets the self-confidence we are supposed to gain in experiencing love and friendship, given that he identifies the gaining of self-confidence with these experiences (ibid., 254). After all, it is possible to dispute the definiteness or the univocal character of love and friendship. In one of his aphorisms, Nietzsche says:

> Not to misunderstand one another in danger – this is what cannot be dispensed with in communication, as is proved by every love affair and every friendship. Nothing of the kind remains the same once the discovery has been made that in using the same words, one of the two parties has feelings, intentions, wishes and fears different from those of the other party. (Nietzsche I, 243)

Honneth confirms his idealizing notion of love in his postdoctoral thesis:

> But because the loved person is certain of the attention he or she receives, he or she can once again find the strength to

open himself or herself up to himself or herself in a relaxed
act of reflection, thus becoming the autonomous subject
with whom the being-one can be experienced as a reciprocal
removal of limits, as a mutual suspension of limitations.
(Honneth II, 105)

Just as one cannot confer upon the experience of love the
definite meaning Honneth ascribes to it in order to develop
his concept of an idealized recognition, one cannot reduce the
experience of friendship to an experience of integral 'reciprocal
recognition'. Silvia Bovenschen shows that friendship cannot
have 'an assigned place in the life-world' or a 'precise discursive
value underpinned by arrangements' (Bovenschen I, 35).

Honneth entrusts himself unreservedly to the idealizing and
ideologizing thrust of his line of argument, transforming it into
the driving force of the argumentation. It is certainly consistent
with such a procedure to identify shame, rage, offence and contempt with 'negative emotional reactions' (Honneth I, 257) which
indicate a 'moral progress' in the struggle for recognition, and
which always contain the possibility of cognitively disclosing the
'injustice suffered'. But how does Honneth intend to justify the
assumption of an always possible translation of emotions into an
intelligibility and an ideality which increasingly dominate history? Honneth knows only of logically preformed and mani-
pulated 'emotional *reactions*', he knows only of an intelligible
negativity, of a negativity which turns into positivity; it seems
that he knows nothing of the dialectically indissoluble tension
Nietzsche has in mind when inscribing love and contempt in a
constellation and speaking of a 'loving contempt' which 'loves
most where it despises most' (Nietzsche II, 239). Do 'conditions
for a successful and undistorted recognition' – do the paths on
which they are established – provide a place and a time for such

contempt, for a contempt which resists the negativity of positive dialectics as much as it resists the idealization of love? Is there indeed any place and any time for '*emotional* reactions' on the way to the establishment of 'conditions for a successful and undistorted recognition'?

It suffices perhaps to emphasize the possibility and even the necessity of all these neglected, ignored, excluded instances of indeterminacy to express doubts as to whether 'conditions for a successful and undistorted recognition' can ever be brought about, or, to put it differently, as to whether it will ever be possible to bridge the 'psychological gaps' which the absence of a particular 'form of social approval' creates in the 'personality' whose identity or whose 'successfully established relationship to itself' are based on an 'intersubjective recognition' (Honneth I, 257). However, an explanation which elucidates the reasons for such neglect, such ignorance and such exclusion, is needed, an explanation which does not simply consist in stating that the author of a 'morality of recognition' did not wish to present a fully developed theory but only to sketch a few principles or 'basic motifs'. The explanation which needs to be given consists in demonstrating that there is an essential link between the reification or objectification of recognition and an idealization which has the effect of an ideologization. It is difficult not to conclude that a politics of recognition which is determined by such a link cannot but produce and reproduce *social conformism*. This conformism is to be understood in a double sense, in a descriptive sense and in the sense of a critique of ideology. A politics of recognition which is oriented towards the primacy of unity and which comprehends the act of recognizing in terms of a presupposition and a result, produces and reproduces social conformism in a descriptive sense, because the creation of 'conditions for a successful and undistorted recognition' marks the completion or the end of a teleological historical process and thereby literally prescribes the conformity of a behaviour. Yet the politics of recognition also produces and reproduces social conformism in the sense of a critique of ideology, because the harmonizing concealment of differences which constantly transform recognition into an act that differs from itself calls for an abstract success and causes the forcible standardization of this act. In truth, the act of recognizing neither succeeds nor fails, but instead triggers the tensions in the struggle for recognition. Shoshana Felman's interpretation of failures or misfires in Austin's theory of speech acts applies to the act of recognizing, too. The failure is not a mere failure, for it effects an opening up: it opens up access to that which is fundamentally blocked. It does not demand recognition, but rescuing, the rescuing of that which is blocked and of that which opens up the access to it by virtue of the very blockage:

> The act of failing thus opens up the space of referentiality – or of impossible reality – not because something is missing, but because something else is done, or because something else is said: the term 'misfire' does not refer to an absence, but to the enactment of a difference. (Felman II, 84)

Like Hegel's speculative concept of recognition, Honneth's conception or reconstruction of a 'morality of recognition' remains tied to the primacy of unity which manipulates recognition in a conformist manner. Honneth takes up arguments from the 'System of Ethical Life' and the Jena *Realphilosophie*. He has good reasons for doing so, since he wants to understand the concept of recognition as an 'intersubjective' concept and keep it free from all 'monological' implications of a 'philosophy of consciousness':

The *Phenomenology of Spirit* allots to the struggle for recognition, once [in the 'System of Ethical Life' and in the *Realphilosophie*] the moral force that drove the process of Spirit's socialization through each of its stages, the sole function of the formation of self-consciousness. Reduced to the single meaning represented in the dialectic of lordship and bondage, the struggle between the subjects fighting for recognition then becomes so closely linked to the practical confirmation experienced in labour that its own particular and stubborn logic disappears almost entirely from the angle of vision. (Honneth II, 62f.)

Yet because Honneth emphasizes and privileges the symmetrical reciprocity in the concept of recognition (ibid., 36f.), because for him the struggle for recognition must ultimately be determined by the 'catalyzing function of a moral provocation' (ibid., 54) and hence by an integrating, forming and 'differentiating' social function, his account hypostasizes the moment of a preceding 'reciprocal or mutual recognition' which is pre-thematic and can be thematized only after the fact. It hypostasizes the moment without which it would remain unclear how the relationship defining a struggle could be established in the first place, as Honneth stresses in the wake of the young Hegel. This hypostasization, this unquestioned presupposition of a recognition which is also meant to be a result, prevents Honneth from recognizing the struggle for life and death in the Jena *Realphilosophie* (ibid., 47), and from actually proposing an approach different from the program of a philosophy of consciousness. He adopts one of Hegel's central conceptions, a conception central to all philosophy of consciousness, the idea of a knowledge of the self as other or of a 'knowing-oneself-in-the-other'. The 'particular and stubborn logic' of recognition also eludes

Honneth's grasp because he is too indebted to the idealistic concept of recognition which Heidegger defines concisely when noting that 'the unconditional [is] that which truly recognizes' (Heidegger III, 184). In the context of a concept of recognition predetermined by idealism, the unconditional is recognized on the grounds of its being the recognizing instance, the instance which externalizes itself and which thereby effectively allows for a letting-be without which nothing conditional could ever relate to it in the struggle for recognition. Even the simple demarcation which separates that which can be thematized from that which cannot, or from that which is pre-thematic, contributes to Honneth's misrecognition of the 'particular and stubborn logic' of recognition. For as something essentially split and divided, recognition can neither be thematized nor can it not be thematized. A pre-thematic recognition, a recognition which cannot be (immediately) thematized, refers to its subsequent thematizability as much as it exceeds it: split, tense, torn apart between a confirmation and an establishment, a heterogeneity and a homogeneity, recognition resists its identification which alone turns it into a theme.

If one does not wish to forgo all conceptual stringency and to let oneself be confused, if one does not wish to confuse others, one must remain attentive to the primacy of unity when reading, for instance, the following sentences:

> In erotic relationships, one *knows* oneself to be reconciled with the other in the sexual union: *no difference* traverses this reconciliation. But the condition of possibility for the *fusion* is always to be found in the opposite experience of encountering the other as a person who continually and repeatedly re-establishes the boundaries of him- or herself. (Honneth II, 105 – emphasis A.G.D.)

159

The 'fusion' Honneth refers to may well be linked to a previous and irrevocable separation ('condition of possibility'), yet the terminological teetering between Kant, Hegel and a certain romantic(izing) ecstasy cannot obscure the fact that what is being acknowledged is immediately revoked and *must* immediately be revoked. How else can a fusion without 'difference' eventuate? The independence, the autonomy, the limitation required by the 'removal of limits and limitations' (ibid.), cannot be what they are meant to be if they are to enable a 'reciprocal being-close-to-oneself in the other' (ibid.). The autonomous existence is such an existence only to the extent that it is directed at its own sublation, at a sublation without difference or without a remainder; it thus serves the purpose of an affirmation of unity. In his own way, Honneth attempts to carry through the program that Ludwig Siep derives from the concept of recognition as a 'principle' of contemporary practical philosophy. According to Siep, it is no longer possible simply to adhere to an idealistic 'teleology'; however, this impossibility leaves untouched the 'fundamental structures of finding oneself again in the other, of affirming oneself and of mutually releasing each other' (Siep, 297), and hence confirms them. But is it possible to stop adhering to an idealistic 'teleology' if union and distance are retained as fundamental structures? Must distance not be subordinated, must the 'immanent aim' (ibid., 284) of a union not be given priority over all other aims if 'finding oneself again in the other' and 'releasing' the self are to be more than purely abstract possibilities?

A politics of recognition which considers recognition to be something presupposed and a result pays the price of an idealization which has the effect of an ideologization, no matter whether it be a selective politics that seeks to forge an exclusive super-culture by means of majoritarian decisions, or a consensual politics that seeks to make facts and norms coincide by means of a discursive activity, or a transposing politics that seeks to translate emotions or affects into the intelligibility of historical progress, thereby securing their inclusion in the discourse. In the light of this conclusion, a clear insight into the approach which refers to itself explicitly as the approach of discourse ethics becomes possible, a clear insight into *the fundamental dependence of discourse ethics on a recognition from which it emerges as a denial or a negation, as the implicit and tacit transformation of recognition into a repeated re-cognition.* There can be no discourse ethics without a 'transcending anticipation' which anticipates, fakes, and simulates the fulfilment of universal claims to validity. There can be no such 'transcending anticipation' without a recognition which awaits its sublation, its transformation into a repeated re-cognition, and which therefore cancels itself out. In discourse ethics, transcendence depends on the immanence of a totality. As a consequence, a critique of discourse ethics, of its necessary confusion of recognition and repeated re-cognition, must be motivated by an anti-dogmatic thought of recognition. It can be summarized in three points:

1. *The confusion of recognition and repeated re-cognition is a confusion of metaphysical and post-metaphysical thinking.*
Discourse ethics claims to be a post-metaphysical way of thinking, since it replaces the 'monological' subjectivity of the philosophy of consciousness with a linguistically mediated, dialogic intersubjectivity which does not presuppose any 'relationship of the self to itself' (Henrich, 502f.). The (regulative) function of the ideality attributed to this intersubjectivity results from a discursive dissolution. The outstanding establishment of an ideal community of communicating agents dissolves the tension between a universal removal of contextual limits and limitations

on the one hand, and the historical, social and life-worldly limits and limitations of contexts on the other. In other words, the instant discourse ethics reaches its aim, the difference between a metaphysical and a post-metaphysical way of thinking can no longer be discerned, given that the (regulative) idea of an ideal community of communicating agents rests on the notion of a complete transparency, a complete appropriation, a complete self-affirmation, just as does the traditional metaphysical concept of the subject. If, to counter such an argument, one highlights the post-metaphysical claim to validity of discourse ethics by hinting at the finitude of the unlimited community of communicating agents, one gets caught in an aporia. For how are limitation and unlimitedness to relate to each other simultaneously? The proponent of discourse ethics does not wish to avoid this aporia or this difficulty by restituting the problematic doctrine of the two worlds, or by subscribing to a metaphysics critical of metaphysics. He therefore exposes himself to the deconstruction of the projective unity which alone guarantees the regulative function of the idea or of the transcendence of a community of communicating agents. The (regulative) idea splits open without ever finding its way back to itself.

2. *The confusion of recognition and repeated re-cognition makes communication turn into illusion.*
If the project propounded by discourse ethics is to succeed, it must postulate that contextuality remains external to the arguments which are recognized and repeatedly re-cognized as true. The necessity of a compromise provoked by the political or moral decision of a majority in a particular context must not affect the 'completeness' or the 'integrity' (Tugendhat, 170f.) of the decontextualized consensus which every true argument is designed to bring about, not if the 'completeness' or the 'integrity'

is conceived of as a (virtual) ultimate certainty, as the grounds for a (virtual) ultimate justification in a community of communicating agents entirely free of limitations and hence entirely unlimited. *Either* there is no exception to there always being a better argument which furthers the decontextualization of communication and allows it to transcend the world – *in which case* communication is nothing but the elimination of its own illusion and ultimately no communication at all: it is 'on the other side' or 'beyond the bounds of language' (Wellmer, 180), beyond this world and with no place in it, a spectre of language. *Or else* there is not always a better argument – *in which case* the pattern of a successful justification we find in discourse ethics, is threatened in its very essence and even deprived of its validity. In both cases, the crucial element of discourse ethics, its concept of an anticipating communication, is loose and adrift. In the first case, discourse ethics presupposes the idealistic primacy of an identity which comprehends all differences within itself, the primacy of a 'unity of reason *in* the diversity of *its* voices'; from a historical angle, this primacy effects an overcoming or a sublation of differences; it effects a 'transcendence from within' which does not have to fear any 'transcendence from without', since the hypothesis of an evil demon never disturbs the possibility of establishing a consensus. In the second case, the recognition of a difference which cannot be sublated or overcome triggers the disintegration of the overarching identity, the disintegration of recognition as presupposition and result. Another way of formulating this criticism of discourse ethics is by objecting to it that it manages to conceive of the relationship between truth and untruth only as an abstract relationship.

Only because in their very essence truth and untruth are not indifferent to each other, only because they belong together, is

163

it possible for a true proposition to become pointedly opposed to the corresponding untrue proposition. (Heidegger IV, 188)

Heidegger's (quasi)proposition is also valid for discourse ethics, even if discourse ethics seems to remain indifferent to the insight that the (quasi)proposition expresses. In fact, the concept of consensual truth has *no relation whatsoever* to the untruth or the invalidity of the arguments dismissed, *while at the same time depending on it*, since a consensus is always determined by its having to be established, by its having to emerge in the course of an argumentation and of a dismissal of untrue or invalid arguments. The paradoxical and unwanted consequence of the indifference of discourse ethics to the relationship between truth and untruth can be phrased as follows: to the extent that the idea of an ideal community of communicating agents (an idea which gives meaning to history) forms the closed horizon of a historical process, of a struggle for recognition of the best of arguments, discourse ethics cannot but present itself as an *apology* of the incomprehensible, the opaque, the untrue, the violent, the arbitrary, the suppressive – as a logodicy. After the fact, every incomprehensible statement, every opaque thought, every untrue or invalid argument, every violent prevention of discursive enlightenment, every arbitrary exclusion of those who participate in the process of argumentation, every suppression of the enlightening truth of discourse caused by counter-enlightenment, will have enabled the establishment of an unlimited communication of communicating agents, for at that stage nothing will have proved to be strong or resistant enough to thwart such an establishment.

3. *The confusion of recognition and repeated re-cognition serves manipulative purposes.*
According to discourse ethics, communication is oriented towards an idea, towards the contradictory idea of an unlimited

and ideal, yet at the same time limited and real community of communicating agents. The approximation to the idea which this definition of communication implies and prescribes, is, however, an ineluctable turning away from the idea, a withdrawal. The more one sticks to the rules of rational argumentation, the more one looks beyond particular contexts, the closer one gets to the others and the more one approaches the ideal community of communicating agents. But this relationship of closeness is determined by a contradiction which is usually overlooked. For every approximation does not only diminish a distance, it also and necessarily causes a withdrawal and a turning away, thus causing the distance to increase. Whatever one is meant to approach is given only as something which withdraws. The specific modality in which an idea is given cannot be simply indifferent to it: if the idea were not affected by its own withdrawal, by a withdrawal which transforms it into an idea in the first place, it would remain entirely out of reach. It could then not be conceived of as an idea which gives meaning and provides an orientation. One cannot approach an idea without simultaneously distancing oneself from it. Controversies, discussions, argumentations lead the ones who participate in them to the debated object only to the extent that they also lead them away from it, especially under conditions which prove to be more or less ideal. For reasons which have nothing to do with empirical difficulties and adversities, the idea of a consensus which is to be established contradicts itself and remains caught up within this contradiction, within a contradiction which produces discontent with the spurious infinity of discussions. Thus both communication and the notion of democracy which depends on the ideal of communication advocated by discourse ethics expose themselves to manipulation and manipulative politics. They are unable to account for this exposure, for this opening-up. Communication as an exchange of arguments which occurs in a supposedly homogeneous medium of argumentative competence, in which the better argument is expected to replace the one previously valid, is an ideology, because it proves to deceive the communicating agents about its inevitable exposure, about the manipulation in the 'spiritual State' (Deleuze/Parnet, 13), of whose philosophical legitimation it partakes.

Plan of life: self-extinguishment

Le croyable, c'est ce qu'on ne voit pas.
Jean-Luc Godard, Numéro deux*

Entre un 'bueno' y otro 'bueno' ¿qué había? Rendijas, intersticios, la raya que no queremos pisar nunca y por cuyo través yo deseaba filtrarme.
Belén Gopegui, La escala de los mapas†

In the period when the 'conditions for a successful and undistorted recognition' have not yet been secured and can only be anticipated in the struggle for recognition, this very anticipation remains inseparable from the question of how the moment of fiction intrinsic to it will affect the secure establishment of those conditions. One can at least say this much: the more pressing the need to anticipate the future conditions and to prefigure the success of recognition in a discursive, affective or expressive man-

---

* 'The believable is what one cannot see.'
† 'What was between one "good" and the other "good"? Clefts, in-between spaces, that borderline we never want to step on and through which I wanted to slip away.'

ner, the greater the danger that the actualization of what is anticipated as a possibility will prove a disappointment – not because not all the expectations can be dealt with, but because the fulfilment of an expectation necessarily dissolves the tension which constitutes it. When the transition to a successful recognition or the instant of its succeeding are thought of as a mere actualization, the fictitious character of the anticipation programs a disappointment. Thus if one were to conceive of the end of the struggle for recognition as a constantly anticipated and presupposed result, as the succeeding of an 'undistorted' recognition, as the establishment of social conditions which correspond to the success of recognition and which manifest it, it would not be possible to conceive of the transition or the passage into these conditions as a mere actualization. One would have to conceive of it as a *transformation*, as the interruption of any anticipation whatsoever. To the extent that the anticipation, the anticipating presupposition, the unavoidable prefiguration, must be interrupted, suspended, avoided; to the extent that it must expose itself to an outside which cannot be determined or anticipated, given that it indicates the limit of all imaginable anticipations and determinations – the (minimal) teleology of a politics of recognition justified by universal pragmatics or discourse ethics participates in the messianic indeterminacy which has left its mark in the motive without motive of the ban on images, of the unspeakable name, of the entirely other, of the erring message in a bottle. The de-position and displacement of the presupposition, the opening up and the exposure of the anticipation, the ex-ception which exempts them both from their determination – emphasize the moment of fiction, the fictitious character of anticipation and presupposition, turning it inside out, as it were. The struggle for recognition as a (minimally) teleological movement of a historical progress is always also a story told between cultures, a self-extinguishment as fiction.

In 'The Switchboard', the second part of his novel *Spiral*, Hans Erich Nossack outlines a peculiar plan of life, a plan of life which consists in pursuing an extinguishment of the self to the point of irreversibility. The figure who bears the 'most common name' and who has a plan encompassing a whole life, can think only of one goal. By 'disappearing into the crowd' without leaving a trace and by inconspicuously concealing his 'belonging', this man wants to reach a point at which the assimilation with the social environment has proved so successful and the fulfilment of others' expectations has left so little space for uncontrollable deviations and accidents, that the danger of a subsequent reintegration and appropriation seems warded off and the disappearance in the 'outside' finally appears to have become possible. The plan of life is pictured as a 'switchboard'. Its operations promise a smooth and total integration. Ultimately, though, they turn against themselves. The functions of the plan or of the board have no other function than the one of a destructive reversal, of a disconnection, of a 'crossing of the border', thereby liberating the self from all functions, all machines, all switchboards, all plans, and leading into a desert, into a polar landscape. In this desert, in this polar landscape, the 'most ordinary word' acquires a dangerous meaning, a 'meaning which annihilates the habitual' (Nossack, 63). The purpose of the plan of life is therefore to neutralize 'weather changes' by depriving the influences of the surroundings of their disturbing effects and by integrating them into the switchboard as new functions. The unknown and the accidental must be transformed into a potential and increase the machine's productivity. The risk which surrenders the plan to unplanned occurrences and which threatens

169

to put the switchboard out of order must become a source which provides additional power and must not result in an irretrievable loss. Even the fundamental transformation triggered by the replacement of the plan of life and the invention of better and more efficient equipment is anticipated in this plan of life and is a component of the switchboard.

In one of those visionary images which are familiar to the readers of Julien Green's early novels, Nossack condenses the unpredictable passage from a revolt which can still be reappropriated and reintegrated, to an eccentricity whose vanishing-line allows for no return. He does so without revealing the meaning of the image. After having broken out of his family for the first and the last time, the son bearing a 'most common name' resists the temptation of committing a murder and thus unwittingly seizes the opportunity that enables him to become a planner. *Does not every plan of life arise out of a recoiling or a withdrawing from an extreme deed, from an expropriating self-transgression* which, in an impossible self-reflection and self-appropriation, appears as the content and the goal of the plan of life thematized in Nossack's 'Switchboard'? The horror of the visionary image is provoked by the inscrutably trivial description of a hair-parting which becomes visible from a perspective gained by coincidence. It is this description, then, that gathers the condensing and concentrating force the image produces:

I simply left him standing and slammed the door behind me. Our room was on the second floor next to the drying-rooms. Halfway down the stairs to the first floor was a landing with a large round window opening onto the garden. There stood a very heavy faience jardiniere, an old-fashioned thing with a plant in it, a rubber tree or an African hemp. The window was open, it was summer, and I stuck my head out. On the balcony below sat my mother with my younger siblings. My father was not there. My mother was sewing or reading the paper. The two little girls were also busy doing something. One could hear their childish talk. A peaceful picture. I saw the hair-partings of the three figures. A white line running over their heads. I shuddered so much that I had to grab hold of the jardiniere. None of them knew that I was up there. Carefully I pulled my head back in. I quietly walked downstairs and left the house. (ibid., 66)

The decision to form a plan of life, which this image anticipates as the unknowingly seized opportunity for a transition, is based on an abandonment and marks the limit of all plans of life. Such a limit becomes especially apparent in the plan of life which consists in the extinguishment of the self. The past, the period of time which precedes the decision to form a plan of life consisting in a self-extinguishment, is extinguished by this very decision, just as the plan extinguishes the incidental events which, as such, cannot be reproduced and thus refuse to let themselves be integrated into it. The past which lies before the decision, and the incidents which cannot be anticipated, are two moments or two elements the plan of life cannot integrate; it must exclude them or include them by exclusion. Hence they endanger the achievement of the chosen aim. The remembrance of the time which precedes the formation of a plan of life is dangerous. Dangerous, too, is the incidental which cannot be controlled from the centre, the external aspects of the path the planner cannot survey and enclose in the internality of his centre of consciousness and agency, the 'aside' whose occurrence is not the occurrence of something important, of something relevant to the plan of life – assuming that something important or relevant is most likely to occur the instant it is perceived as irrelevant or unimportant

(Frey, 87). Dangerous is the im-pertinence, the lack of belonging, the uncanny discrepancy between the inconspicuousness which finally turns into complete indifference, and the assimilation which consists in the recognition of a belonging: this discrepancy can lead to a sudden exclusion from the 'frame of the habitual' and create a 'gap' which prevents the planner from entirely giving himself over to the thing he is dealing with, or from becoming entirely absorbed 'in the thing'. Dangerous is the death the planner must die if he does not want to dispute the other's place in life and thereby distance himself from his namelessness: for no one has to be more alive and more vigilant than this dead person whose mask must not grow together with his faceless face. Dangerous is the transformation of the plan of life into a 'novel', a 'surprising plot', a 'fate' which gains power over the planner.

Hence the planner does not leave the centre of society in order to reach its outer limits and free himself from it. He does not want to destroy it from outside, regardless of whether he once belonged to it, or whether he never was a member of it. Rather, the planner seeks the negative freedom of the ironist; he seeks a refusal to recognize within recognition; he seeks a disconnection within a connection; he seeks the eccentric in the centre, in the infinite approximation of the centre to the centre and in the infinite distancing of the centre from the centre, in the centre's terrible defencelessness and in its almost imperceptible misery. In her essay 'In Praise of the Nuance', Silvia Bovenschen reveals the particularity of such an eccentricity. She distinguishes it from the 'standardized deviation' of conformism and sees it as a movement in which 'extreme expansion' and 'absolute contraction', 'plenitude and emptiness' seem to coincide (Bovenschen II, 62). It is as if the planner continued to fulfil his social functions while remaining free of all external demands and entering the 'black body' which absorbs everything and gives nothing back, the body to which Valéry compares the surplus of a pure, simple, impersonally present consciousness. The personality is compelled to engage in recognition (Valéry, 1226), but the intellectual human being strives to attain the infinitely detached and hence inexhaustible power which lies in his consciousness and which he can attain only by means of an uncompromising refusal of everything personal and of recognition. This power is the immortal potentiality of consciousness, a pure or mere relationship, a relationship between nothing and nothing which, as Derrida stresses in his essay on Valéry, is barely a relation (Derrida III, 282). The abstract freedom granted by the potentiality and denied by the actuality is anticipated in the shadowy peace the planner finds before fully carrying out his plan:

> [I] sit unmoved in the scheme, in my shadowy figure, and can relax. My silence remains untouched. Today there is no longer any need for me to contemplate, to think about something, to make an exhausting detour via the brain. It has become a function. I behave and speak the way they want me to behave and speak. (Nossack, 73)

At this point it remains undecided whether the fulfilment of the plan of life depends on an improvement which endows its anticipation with the permanency of a stable state of affairs, or whether such a fulfilment cannot be anticipated at all: in the latter case, that which is yet to come would not even present itself as the disfigured figure of a shadowy figure, of a shadowy figure of the shadowy figure, of a poverty of experience which excludes all richness.

However, the fact that the planner reveals his plan; that he seems to detect a similarity between his plan and someone else's life; that he discusses his plan with someone else and wishes to establish a common link which cannot be established – all this indicates that the plan must still be improved and that a plan of life is required in order to pursue the chosen plan of life. But once the plan of life splits into two plans of life, it exposes itself to the contingency of a double decision or a double instant. The decision to pursue a plan of life that discloses the possibility of pursuing a plan of life must remain as external to the plans of life as must the instant at which they have come so close to each other that they touch each other in the immediacy of a transition or a passage, with the final plan of life replacing the provisional plan of life. Every self-extinguishment that does not result from a plan of life can be justified by society; every self-extinguishment that consists in a plan of life must be induced or instigated by a decision. These two extremes limit the possibility of self-extinguishment. By paying attention to the narrator's remarks, the reader can recognize the impossibility of establishing a community of those who plan their self-extinguishment. The planner who reveals his plan, because he seems to have detected a similarity, talks only to himself; he transforms the one he addresses into a narrator, into a required and yet rejected witness, into the 'accidental pretext' for a monologue, into an element whose contingency allows him to break the conversation off at random and still raise the question around which it revolves. Thus, it is the monologue; it is the self-referential relationship expressed in the form of a monologue by the autonomous will of a subject guided by a maxim; it is the self's testimony to itself, a testimony which already implies alterity and includes the excluded narrator, that points to the fact that the self's extinguishment has not yet occurred and that the transition to the final plan of life has still to be effected. In retrospect, this view is ratified at the beginning of the story when the narrator wonders what may have become of the planner.

As one can see, carrying out a plan of life which consists in the self's extinguishment, both in the sense of a plan aiming for such an extinguishment and in the sense of a plan which allows for an extinguished self to exist, means encountering a barrier which cannot be removed and which, paradoxically, is also the condition of possibility of such an enterprise. On the one hand, the chosen and pursued plan of life must maintain the difference between functionality and a-functionality, between recognition and the refusal to recognize, between the outer and the inner. Without this difference, self-extinguishment cannot be distinguished from mere assimilation, from the assimilation of those who have been recognized by society. On the other hand, however, the difference which self-extinguishment needs to succeed, and which the plan of life needs in order to let itself be carried out, triggers a tension which leads to a repeated postponement of the transition from a provisional to a final plan of life, and to a perpetuated anticipation of the success of the pursuit. Thus the difference promises the self-extinguishment it also impedes. The planner must continuously reassure himself by establishing that he is different from the ones who, having been recognized, assimilate into their surroundings. He is always tempted to interpret the external aspect of a sign which alone provides a possibility of re-cognizing a recognition and a refusal to recognize. He can never interrupt his monologue once and for all.

Does 'The Switchboard' shed light on the project which postulates the creation of conditions for a 'successful' and 'undistorted' recognition? Does the text convey a better understanding of the anticipation effected by such a project?

One can maintain that there is no plan of life which does not contain a plan of life leading up to a plan of life, a plan of life for a plan of life. Plans of life presuppose plans of life whose aim or goal is the creation and conservation of conditions under which the execution of a plan of life does not break the rules which must, at least ideally, be valid for all plans of life. As is well known, John Rawls has dealt with the question of good and rational plans of life in his *Theory of Justice*. Rawls starts out from the assumption that every human being lives his life in view of a goal or an aim, and therefore carries out a more or less long-term plan of life. It is precisely the pursuit of a long-term plan of life which includes short-term plans that is supposed to define life as a human one. Even the limit case of a decision which rejects the establishment of a plan of life is interpreted by Rawls in the context of his definition of a human life. A universal claim is linked to it, a claim which transcends the singularity and particularity of cultures and which can never be reduced to a specific cultural implication: 'But in fact the question of what to do with our life is always there, although some societies force it upon us more obviously than others and at a different time of life' (Rawls, 413).

Rawls investigates the rationality of plans of life. On the one hand, he measures it against the 'principles of rational choice': against the efficacy of the means necessary to carry it out, against the extent of a plan in comparison with another plan, against the probability of reaching the intended aim by pursuing a particular plan. On the other hand, he measures it against the kind of choice-making which is guided by 'deliberative rationality'. Hence the best and most rational plan proves to be the one a human being chooses because he has 'full information' at his disposal, because he can do away with 'incorrect beliefs' and 'misconceptions', because he can secure his decision or his choice on the basis of a precise knowledge of the consequences it entails. Yet Rawls does not elucidate what it is that provokes the choice of the best and most reasonable or rational plan of life; after all, for such a choice, for such a decision, the anticipation and the anticipated already coincide. What role does that which opposes rationality play when a decision is made upon which the rationality of a plan of life, and the rational behaviour of the human being defined by it, both depend? Rawls assumes that human activity and human thought strive to satisfy an innate need to achieve a higher order; this is why long-term plans of life must be preferred. They demand a 'more complex combination of abilities' and have to be regarded as a greater challenge to the human being. But is the most inclusive and complex plan of life not always a plan of life which consists in self-extinguishment, in the extinguishment described in 'The Switchboard'? Does the highest degree of self-respect not lie in the carrying out of a plan of life which consists in self-extinguishment, in the extinguishment which leaves social institutions intact and nevertheless gives the subject enough space to exist in accordance with the most fundamental liberty, the most conciliatory and the most ineffable liberty? Only such a plan includes all other plans and adds another goal or aim to them: the goal or aim of self-extinguishment; only such a plan demands a 'combination of abilities' more complex than the one required by other plans, given that it doesn't omit any other plan and includes an additional aim or goal: it is the paradigm of the formula n + 1. The bourgeois ideology of rise and advancement, the binding together of the 'results and enjoyments of an entire life into one coherent structure' (ibid., 421), terminates in self-extinguishment. One could object to this thesis by asserting that self-extinguishment as goal or aim is 'meaningless' (ibid., 419). The objection may be countered by showing that true self-realization can only be achieved in self-extinguishment, if self-realization is the aim of a plan of life and if it resides in the self's realization of the highest possible order.

Doubtless it is 'perfectly rational' to pursue a useful and 'satisfactory' plan, a plan which is not the best, a plan whose ascending

177

line or trajectory is not the steepest, since the time for consideration, choice and decision is necessarily limited and finite. Rawls even believes that there is nothing 'irrational in an aversion to deliberation itself, provided that one is prepared to accept the consequences' (ibid., 418) of decisions taken without reflection, and thus behave as a 'rational person' who does not regret her decisions in hindsight. But as the plan becomes more long-term and rational; as it demands more abilities; as the combination of abilities required proves more complex; and as the amount or period of time a responsible decision may dispose of diminishes, precisely because the risks of a possible criticism increase and turn out to be confusing and almost uncontrollable – the danger of 'momentary temptations and distractions', which impede the chosen plan to be carried out, becomes greater, and both the continuity of human life and the unity of its supposed rationality are more and more threatened. Without this tension which traverses the plan of life and breaks it open; without the constitutive dependency of the rational upon something which cannot be unified, which remains discontinuous, irrational, meaningless and aimless, which cannot be resolved into continuity, unity, rationality and meaningful planning – life would be stillborn, a life that could not be lived at all. It would not be a coherent and consistent context of 'the activities of one rational subject spread out over time' (ibid., 420).

The irrational element of a planned and rational human life blocks the transition from one plan of life to the other; it prevents a plan of life from being carried out completely and thereby creating a passage to another plan of life, to the plan of life itself, as it were. If, however, the execution of an already rational plan of life had managed to establish conditions which allowed for each future execution of a plan of life to be rational without exception, then the conditions for a 'successful' and 'undistorted' recognition would have been brought about and their supratemporal permanence would be guaranteed. The social subjects would have reached a degree of self-confidence which would let them express the recognition or 'appreciation of others' (ibid., 441) with undiminished liberty. To the extent that conditions for a 'successful' and 'undistorted' recognition are conditions for pursuing and executing rational plans of life; to the extent that they know of no exception to such a pursuit and such an execution, they posit the 'frame of the habitual' as an absolute. They are defined in such a way that anything that would stand outside this frame remains irrelevant to them. Hence they touch a limit of recognition and converge with a form of self-extinguishment. The only difference which can still continue to exist under such circumstances; the only difference which the 'frame of the habitual' cannot include within itself, is the difference between pure actuality and pure potentiality, between pure functionality and pure a-functionality, between pure recognition and a pure refusal to recognize. As has become clear, this difference can be regarded as the condition of possibility and impossibility of a self-extinguishment which does justice to its paradoxical concept, i.e. which is neither a simple self-extinguishment nor a conservation which reintegrates the extinguished into a given frame, but the extinguishment of a self. Yet if the difference between pure recognition and a pure refusal to recognize or a pure de-cognition continues to exist, the conditions for a 'successful' and 'undistorted' recognition suffer an unusual and incommensurable postponement which holds them hovering in undecidability, between success and failure.

Consequently, it is not only the necessary interruption of the anticipation of an achieved recognition that produces fictions. That which is anticipated reveals itself to be a fiction of self-extinguishment. It in turn produces fictions, given that the difference between pure recognition and pure de-cognition, without which self-extinguishment extinguishes itself and becomes a fiction of self-extinguishment, thwarts self-extinguishment. Can 'The Switchboard', a text which is created by that which creates fictions (of self-extinguishment), a text which revolves around it, be read as nothing but (a) fiction?

THE CULTURE OF INTERPRETATION

Struggling for recognition

Hegel's dialectical treatment of the concept of recognition demands particular consideration, as Charles Taylor recognizes. In
a footnote he refers to the famous chapter on lordship and bondage in the *Phenomenology of Spirit* (Taylor, 36). This chapter is
important for any discussion that deals with recognition, since it
elucidates the necessarily contradictory nature of recognition's
movement, the one-sidedness and the reciprocity which mark
the act of recognizing. Of course, this is not to imply that all
social philosophers who focus on the concept of recognition and
take Hegel as their point of departure concern or need to concern themselves primarily with this particular chapter.

To the extent that it is a dialectical movement, a movement of
determination through opposition and mediation, the movement
of recognition establishes a continuity between different moments
of consciousness. It leads from a consciousness which has not yet
been recognized, because it has not proved itself in the struggle
for recognition, to a self-consciousness which is essentially determined by the result of this struggle, by the actual state of being
recognized. Consciousness constitutes itself in the struggle for
recognition as a free, identical and certain self-consciousness
existing in and for itself. According to the paragraph on the

struggle for recognition which, in the *Encyclopaedia*, takes up the main points of the *Phenomenology*, this continuous and unified movement describes the passage from the natural condition to society and the state. In bourgeois society and under the rule of law, one is always already recognized as a person:

> There man is recognized and treated as a *rational* being, as *free*, as a person; and the individual, on his side, makes himself worthy of this recognition by overcoming the natural state of his self-consciousness and obeying a *universal*, the will that is *a will in and for itself*, the *law*; he behaves, therefore, towards others in a manner that is *universally valid*, recognizing them – as he wishes others to recognize him – as free, as persons. (Hegel I, 172f.)

The resultant and true state of being recognized without which culture, society and the state could not be formed and could not 'differentiate' themselves, emerges from the struggle for recognition which is and must be a struggle for life and death. Thus, Hegel's assertion in the *Phenomenology* that an individual who has not risked his life can 'be recognized as a person even though he himself does not attain the truth of being recognized as an independent self-consciousness', may also be applied to the presentation of recognition in the *Encyclopaedia*. Gadamer calls this assertion 'remarkable' and interprets it in a similar way when he maintains that Hegel is alluding to the fact that the legal system alone is unable to guarantee any 'real self-consciousness' (Gadamer II, 71). The struggle for recognition in the course of which self-consciousness reaches its independence, autonomy and freedom, is a movement of truth and does not only require us to distinguish between an untrue recognition and a true recognition which results from the movement of self-consciousness. We must equally distinguish between the one-sided, incomplete, improper state of being recognized, and the complete, proper, truly reciprocal recognition which indicates that truth is finally for and in self-consciousness.

What elements, what conceptual configurations which reveal themselves to be indispensable to a concept of recognition inscribed in the context of a philosophy of consciousness, and which may not just depend on the specificity of this context, can one abstract from the dialectical presentation of what consciousness knows by knowing itself?

1. Recognition is *always* a movement of self-consciousness, of a consciousness which seeks satisfaction and as a desiring consciousness cannot find it. Mere desire relates only negatively to its object and infinitely reproduces it as an independent object, thus infinitely reproducing itself. If there is no recognition without self-consciousness, if every act of recognition is linked to a certain self-consciousness, then there is also no self-consciousness without recognition: recognition is always a satisfaction which transcends desire. Whoever does nothing but desire is incapable of recognizing and thinking. Only recognition as the result of a struggle for recognition leads to a free, thinking self-consciousness. It is precisely for this reason, it is because desire and recognition designate different stages in the movement of self-consciousness, that it is possible to conceive of a link between recognition and love. In his lectures on the philosophy of art, Hegel defines love as recognition, as a recognition which is 'real and total' the moment the ones who recognize each other are 'for themselves in a fulfilled and accomplished unity' (Hegel II, 562).

2. Recognition, by means of which self-consciousness constitutes itself in its truth, is *always* a relationship between one self-consciousness and another self-consciousness. For the other

183

who remains other and maintains his independence untouched, the other who in his very otherness has thwarted all repeated re-cognition, cannot be recognized at all. In Hegel's words, the independent or autonomous object of self-consciousness 'must carry out this negation of itself in itself' (Hegel III, 109). It must become for the other what it is unto itself, namely something negative *in* itself. The desiring consciousness has merely an incomplete and conditional certainty of itself; it must orient itself constantly to the desired object and annihilate it, since this annihilation never succeeds in affecting the independence of its object, of that which is annihilated. By contrast, the doubled self-consciousness, both recognizing and recognized, is a consciousness which, instead of vainly seeking its satisfaction in desire, realizes itself in the form of an unconditionally certain unity: its reality or actuality is the 'unity of itself in its otherness' (ibid., 110). Thus, recognition proves to be spiritual in essence, if spirit is the name for an 'absolute substance' which reconciles every self-consciousness that exists for itself with another self-consciousness, preserving its 'complete freedom and independence': 'An *I* that is a *We*, and a *We* that is an *I*'.

3. Recognition is *always* contradictory because it comprises a twofold obligation. It comprises two demands whose incompatibility exposes recognition and the cognitive identification of its contradiction to an outside that must remain inaccessible to all cognition. For if recognition is to be more than an always already presupposed state of being recognized which is included in the constituted or cultivated totality of society, the state and the legal system, then it must not exclude anything. It must exclude that which excludes. This is the first demand. Hegel underlines its decisive character for recognition in his *System of Speculative Philosophy* from 1803 and 1804, by stating that 'everyone [must] discern from the other whether he is an absolute consciousness'

or not, and 'place himself in relation to the other in such a way that this may come about'. In the *Phenomenology of Spirit*, Hegel emphasizes the unconditionality of a self-consciousness which presents itself or which unfolds its own process of constitution. He thereby attracts our attention to the exclusion of exclusion which constitutes the act of recognizing. Recognition is impossible if self-consciousness clings to something external, to a conditioning, limiting, excluding outside which restricts the unconditionality of self-consciousness by impeding the exclusion of exclusion. Self-consciousness must abstract from everything that defines the determinacy of its totality; it must thus posit itself absolutely or as an absolute, and exclude exclusion. It must negate the other self-consciousness because at first it is a 'simple being for itself'. In its immediacy, it is nothing but self-same. Its only relationship to the other amounts to the negativity of a pure exclusion:

> The *presentation* of itself, however, as the pure abstraction of self-consciousness consists in showing itself as the pure negation of its objective form, or in showing that it is not attached to any specific *existence*, to the individuality common to existence as such, to life. (ibid., 113)

Only by finally excluding itself and the other, the being-outside-itself, can an individual self-consciousness assert and affirm itself in its 'simple being-for-itself' and let itself be recognized. This, then, is the second demand. A self-consciousness which has abstracted from everything determinate demands recognition, for without recognition, it could never be certain of its self-certainty. *On the one hand the self-certainty of self-consciousness depends on an exclusion which seeks to exclude exclusion itself; yet, on the other hand, it dissolves and vanishes if, by excluding exclusion*

185

and negating the other self-consciousness, self-consciousness is not recognized and perpetuates exclusion.

As a consequence of the assertion or affirmation of recognition, which is an assertion or affirmation of the one who recognizes and which cannot be avoided, recognition limits that which is to be recognized and hence also itself. It does not deserve to be called recognition; it exposes that which is to be recognized to its nullity. As a consequence of the exclusion of exclusion which renders an unrestricted and unconditional recognition possible – the only recognition that deserves its name – recognition is excluded, as is that which is to be recognized and which is nullified if it is not recognized. Hegel takes the contradictory, paradoxical nature of recognition to its logical conclusion. If *it is to be possible* for an act of recognition to take place, then it must take place in a struggle of recognition which *must* be a 'struggle for life and death'.

Is this impossible struggle, which perhaps cannot be brought to an end, or which perhaps does not end with a result, a struggle which has a right to bear its name? In his lectures on Nietzsche, Heidegger speaks of a 'genuine struggle'. He seems to distinguish between different kinds of struggle and to gauge the genuineness of a struggle from the unlimited character of a reciprocal escalation: 'But the genuine struggle is the one in which those who struggle excel, first the one then the other, and in which power for such excelling unfolds within them' (Heidegger V, 158).

For Hegel, there are three possibilities for a struggle to end. A struggle ends when one of the two fighters falls prey to the 'abstract negativity' of death. Has a struggle actually taken place in this case? A struggle ends when one of the two fighters stops fighting at the boundaries of 'abstract negativity'. Has a struggle taken place in this other case? Finally, a struggle ends when one of the two fighters exhausts the force which sustains it by bringing about a dialectical result. Has a struggle taken place in the case of such an ultimate reversal?

Recognition is *always* involved in a struggle, the struggle for recognition is *always* a struggle for life and death, an impossible struggle. This is why periodizations and chronological gradations such as the ones proposed by Hegel, or differentiations between a presocial natural condition and conditions of labour, formation and culture, encounter a limit which makes it difficult to conceive of the struggle for recognition as a forming dialectical process, as a transition from nature to culture, and to attribute it a unique and determinate place. The fact that one can and cannot be recognized as a person, hints at the difficulties inherent in such an attribution.

To assign the struggle for recognition its proper place is all the more difficult since it itself seems to be submitted to an uncontrollable historical dynamic in and through which the progress of history turns against itself and against its speculative dialectical determination. In his essay on Beckett's *Endgame*, Adorno writes:

> The Hegelian dialectic of lordship and bondage [the struggle for recognition] is not presented in accordance with the conventions of traditional aesthetics, rather, it is ridiculed. The servant is no longer capable of taking charge and doing away with domination. The mutilated Clov would scarcely be capable of it, and in any case, according to the historico-philosophical sundial of the play it is too late for spontaneous action. There is nothing left for Clov to do but wander off into the world that does not exist for these recluses, with the prospect of probably dying there. He cannot even rely on his freedom to die. To be sure, he does resolve to part and enters as if to say good-bye [. . .] But we do not witness him exit; he halts by the door and stays there, 'impassive and motionless, his eyes fixed on Hamm, till the end'. This is an allegory

187

whose intention has fizzled out. Aside from differences which may be decisive but also completely irrelevant, it is identical with the beginning. No spectator *and no philosopher* would be in a position to maintain that the play is not starting all over again. The pendulum of the dialectic has come to a standstill. (Adorno V, 269 – emphasis A.G.D.)

How is the dialectic to move forward in the course of a progression; how is the struggle for recognition to be a step in such a dialectical progression; how is a philosopher or a poet to represent this progression – if decisive distinctions no longer have a decisive effect? Does the word 'struggle' sound anachronistic in integrally rationalized societies because of its epic dimension, its rootedness in a natural element? Does rationalization end up transforming the rudiments of this natural element into a comic and indifferent echo?

Every recognition which lacks unconditionality or which does not show the trace of a struggle is merely a formal assurance, just as every recognition which results from the struggle for recognition is liable to lose its force. It is not by chance that, both in the fragmentary *System of Speculative Philosophy* and in the *Encyclopaedia*, Hegel points out that 'words, assurances, threats or promises' are not sufficient for recognition to take place, and that self-consciousness acquires the 'capability for freedom' involved in recognition through the 'danger of death', not through simple assurance. It is not by chance either that Hegel justifies war with the argument that a long or even eternal peace leads to a politically dangerous 'solidification'. Even Frantz Fanon, who writes about the recognition of black men in the Antilles and discusses it in the light of the dialectic of lordship and bondage, reproaches the French colonial masters for interrupting dialectics and failing to carry through the struggle. Because black men were recognized by white men without any conflict, because they had to move from one way of life to another way of life without being allowed to move from one life to another life, the possibility of true recognition was stripped away from them, and dependence and domination were perpetuated under the guise of recognition. Thus Fanon underlines the necessity and risk of a dangerous struggle (*ébranlement de la mort* – convulsions of death, *dissolution irréversible* – irreversible dissolution) wherever a true act of recognition is supposed to take place (Fanon, 218). *We're queer, we're here, so get fuckin' used to it*: in the context of this slogan, this outcry, this outrage, the unconditional and combatant character of recognition resides in the fact that the ones who demand to be recognized cannot be content with a recognition that turns them into mere 'persons', thereby integrating them into an existing system. The recognition claimed must shatter and transform the system. If the demand for recognition regards recognition as a task, as something to be achieved or as something to be resolved by means of a discourse; if it abandons recognition to the impotence of argumentation, of a task or an obligation, then the struggle for recognition which is not a task but a praxis, and which cannot be identified with a simple fulfilment of a claim by means of an application of ethical prescriptions and rational criteria of argumentation, aims for the establishment of a lasting state of affairs.

One cannot assure the other that one recognizes him. Hence, whenever one attempts to analyse the act of recognizing as a linguistically conventionalized act, one must also be aware of its incompatibility with language, at least if language is understood as a regulated system comprising fixed meanings and standardized acts. The discourse can grasp recognition only belatedly. The speechlessness of recognition escapes the legitimating conceptual discourse which recognition makes possible in the first place. If one takes the progressive development of thought in the *Phenomenology* and the results of its 'practical experiences' (Siep, 213) seriously, thinking whose object moves in a conceptual element, rather than in a 'pictorial and figurative' one, is dependent on a recognition by means of which self-consciousness fights for its freedom. Does not Kierkegaard, too, refer to the speechlessness of the language of recognition when, in the 'Ultimatum' which concludes the second part of *Either/Or*, he considers the idea that humans are always in the wrong when relating to God, and traces it back to the force of love, rather than to the power of thought? The recognition or the acknowledgement of God and the certainty of divine truth should not be confused with the result of a series of operations of the reflective mind. The moment the idea of constant wrong is grasped and made explicit as a thought, it must be interpreted as a belated objectification which betrays the force of the indubitable immediacy Kierkegaard attributes to love.

Politics is a politics of recognition to the extent that self-consciousness, identity, difference, culture, society, the state and the legal system cannot be formed and thought without recognition, whatever one's concept of recognition may be. But does not the highlighting of an irreconcilable contradiction in the act of recognizing end up delivering politics to an activity which is legitimated by a form of social Darwinism and which conceals social antagonisms? Does the notion of a struggle determined by such a contradiction not lead to a hypostasization of domination? Does it not glorify domination by glorifying the (real or deferred) death of those who are transfigured into heroic fighters? Is the logic of a politics based on a recognition which keeps provoking a struggle for life and death, not the logic of a sacrificial death which serves the purposes of domination or which points towards the immanentism of a community whose members re-cognize and find themselves at its borders, in a death meant to secure the unity and uniformity of the whole? Does a politics of recognition which follows this logic not apologetically maintain the existing conditions and nihilistically stifle any revolutionary impulse? To give unequivocally affirmative answers to these questions means to jump to conclusions, to turn recognition into a result, into a state of being recognized, and to bind the effects of the struggle for recognition, both disintegrative and integrative, to the sole goal of integration. For the questions raised presuppose an already established order, an order which can be shattered by a crisis only to the extent that its securing powers or forces are provided with even greater and more plentiful resources. Recognition as a constitutive moment in the constitution of self-consciousness, identity, difference, culture, society, the state and the legal system, must be deconstructed, it must be pushed to its very limits.

4. Since, if one sticks to its paradigmatic conceptual treatment in Hegel, recognition can become what is meant by its concept only in a struggle for life and death; since recognition is permeated and torn apart by a double task or obligation which, by virtue of its doubling, is incompatible with itself; since asymmetry, imbalance, dissimilarity and heterogeneity belong to recognition as much as homogeneity and balancing reciprocity; since, when it first emerges, recognition is *always* embedded in a destabilizing tension; since recognition is not stable and balanced, and does not maintain itself in a middle which holds the extremes together and preserves them from being deconstructed; since recognition cannot immediately posit itself in its proper conceptual form or figure – the end which allegedly brings the struggle for recognition to its conclusion, is *always* a provisional end. Recognition, as that which is supposed to result from a struggle and put an end to it, is *always* an improper, dissimilar,

191

one-sided recognition, a recognition which falls short of its 'demanded meaning' or its 'required significance', and is exposed to disintegration.

But how is a provisional end brought about? A provisional end is brought about by a transformation. The 'abstract negativity' of death which releases those who were involved in the struggle as mere things, denying them once and for all the opportunity of giving and receiving themselves 'through consciousness', is transformed into the (absolute) 'negation of consciousness' which sublates or '*supersedes* in such a way as to *preserve* and *maintain* what is superseded', and which 'consequently survives its own supersession' (Hegel III, 114f.). This can also be put differently. In the struggle for recognition, the one who is incapable of enduring the vicinity of death and who virtually re-cognizes the impossibility of doing justice to the double task or obligation of recognition is the one who shrinks back from death. Hence, the struggle ends provisionally with the dependence of the retreating self-consciousness on the self-consciousness which has proved to be more daring. Self-consciousness pays a price for its retreating, given that it must renounce its being-for-itself and recognize the other self-consciousness which it has saved from perishing by preserving its own life. Thus the recognized self-consciousness turns out to depend on the retreating self-consciousness because without the other's retreating it would have committed 'suicide': 'It appears to him as consciousness that it seeks the *death* of the other; but it is provoking its own death; it is suicidal by exposing itself to such *danger*' (Hegel IV, 211).

The dependence of the master on the slave which arises because the slave has saved the master's life, is not mentioned in the *Phenomenology*. It is expressed with the precision of a psycho-analytical terminology in an interpretation of the dialectic of lordship and bondage proposed by Judith Butler: 'The lord cannot deny his body through suicide, so he proceeds *to embody his denial*' (Butler, 53). The relationship between master and slave, one could say following Hegel, is not a historical invariant because the struggle continues underground. It is not a historical invariant because the slave, the dependent and recognizing self-consciousness, has perceived, deferred, stored, steered, channelled and instrumentalized the negativity in the fear of death, in the fear of the 'absolute master', and because the lack of autonomy, the dependence on a feared other and the fettering to a thing to be worked on, holds within itself the power of making oneself autonomous, of coming into one's own, of appropriating meaning. Finally, the relationship between master and slave is not a historical invariant because the 'demanded meaning' or the 're-quired significance' of recognition implies an impossible double task, *and* the establishment of reciprocity, equality, homogeneity and symmetry. In the light of a demand of meaning which can be fulfilled, in the 'spiritual daylight of the present', what is improper, 'one-sided and unequal' may appear as the cunning of reason, a cunning by means of which recognition strives to constitute itself *as* recognition.

The deferral of death which creates the dialectical relationship between master and slave, the economy of death which results from the withdrawal of a self-consciousness forced back into itself and from a self-preservation through recognition, forms the basis for revolutionary discourses which refer to Hegel. At the same time, though, it also triggers a radical criticism which reveals the fundamentally conservative trait of revolutions justified in terms of a dialectic.

In his lectures on Hegel's philosophy, Alexandre Kojève suggests that one can actually comprehend this philosophy as a 'true anthropology' (Kojève, 573). Hegel's philosophy is called an anthropology because speculative dialectics must be freed from its monistic misunderstanding of itself, and limited to the 'analysis of human or historical existence', to an inquiry into 'human reality', into a reality which arises from 'an act of progressive temporal self-creation' and which therefore consists of a transformative activity. Labour transforms the form of the 'natural world' and discloses a 'cultural world' in which human self-consciousness can re-cognize itself repeatedly. Such an activity is, however, a negativity; it is a behaviour which relates to death. Kojève comments on the passage from the preface to the *Phenomenology*, in which Hegel speaks of a 'tarrying with the negative', attributing to it 'magical power':

> Human beings create their human essence or being by transforming nothingness as if through 'magical power'. They transform the nothing they themselves are, the nothing that presents itself to them and that they reveal once they are dead, turning it into the negating existence of the fighter and the worker who both engender history. The 'tarrying' with death realizes negativity and integrates it into the natural world in the form of a being that is essentially human. (ibid., 549)

It follows from this passage that there are two reasons which justify the anthropological determination of (speculative) dialectics: the necessary limitation of its scope to the 'cultural world' created by the fighting and working human being, and the finitude human beings must be aware of if they are to create a culture. Indeed, Kojève defines Hegel's philosophy as a philosophy of death. He defines absolute knowledge as a 'conscious acceptance of death, of a death which must be understood as a total and final annihilation' (ibid., 540). Outside the 'cultural world' human beings are 'purely nothing', within it they differ from such nothingness only 'for a certain amount of time' (ibid., 575).

In a footnote, Kojève explains that, placing himself in the tradition of Hegel, Marx retained the motives of struggle and labour, developing an essentially 'historical' philosophy. However, Marx is said to have neglected the 'theme of death' on which Heidegger then focused, only to fail in taking up the motives of struggle and labour. It is quite obvious that, when conceiving of a culturalistic economy of death, Kojève pursues a line of argument Freud had pursued before him; for in *Beyond the Pleasure Principle* and also in an article on the 'economic problem of masochism', Freud leaves no doubt as to the necessity of interpreting life and culture as 'detours on the path to death'. Both ultimately owe their existence to 'variable mixtures and amalgamations' of life- and death-drives.

In Kojève's view, (speculative) dialectics is a true anthropology or the truth of all anthropology because human beings can defer death and transform 'abstract negativity' into productivity only if they succeed in not succumbing to the abstract character of death. A human being who resists death within death, has a knowledge of death, he knows how to die. By willingly confronting and enduring it, human beings 'realize' death, they 'achieve' it and prove themselves to be 'a death conscious of itself' (ibid., 572).

Kojève's extensive introduction does not, however, resolve the question of how the notion of a 'true anthropology' can be reconciled with the notion of an end of history, of an end on which the very possibility of a philosophical exposition of a 'true anthropology' depends. Is Kojève not forced to revoke the limitation of speculative dialectics which restricts it to the human or 'cultural world'? While on the one hand he asserts that the disappearance of mankind at the end of a dialectical and historical progress is no 'cosmic catastrophe', given that the 'natural world' persists in its indifferent immutability and that the posthistorical human being lives on as an animal in harmony with nature, on the other hand he affirms that, against all expectations, the post-historical age is 'specifically human'. He believes to have discerned its signs during a trip to Japan in the early sixties (ibid., 436f.). Of the philosopher or the sage who, in post-history, is content with understanding everything, never negating or changing anything, Kojève says that his life is not a historical and free one, though 'truly human' (ibid., 563).

Speculative dialectics as 'true anthropology' presents history as the history of the working servant or slave. For the revolutionary abolition of lordship and bondage, of mastery and slavery, is reserved for the slave. It is thus for the slave alone that a future opens up. The master has transcended the given world by exposing himself and risking his life, but he has not done so by working, by inhibiting his desire, by bringing disappearance and vanishing to a hold, by (trans)forming the object. Kojève concludes that, unlike the slave, the master is only able to 'realize' his freedom in death (ibid., 34) and that for this reason, he remains fettered to a given world as long as he is alive. The master destroys himself, he is destroyed by the fact that he who has become what he sought to become, can only ever be himself. This conclusion is intended to remain within the boundaries of Kojève's presentation of the dialectic of lordship and bondage that we find in the *Phenomenology*. Perhaps it appears no longer to be a pertinent conclusion when we turn to the *Encyclopaedia*, in which it is not just the slave who abolishes lordship and bondage:

On the other hand, the fact that master and slave *share* needs as well as concern for their satisfaction, and the intuition of the suspension of the immediate individual will which the slave objectifies for him, make the self-consciousness of the master realize that in such a suspension or sublation lies his own truth, too; they make it submit its own selfish will to the law of the will that exists in and for itself. (Hegel I, 176)

To the extent that the master must destroy himself, every master is his own slave and helplessly at the mercy of the slave who is under his control. Resentment seems to be inscribed in the dialectical relationship between lordship and bondage.

Kojève makes the revolution dependent on the productive overcoming of the abstract negativity of death which takes place in the struggle for recognition. In his lecture on Hegel, death and sacrifice, Georges Bataille, who explicitly refers to Kojève's elucidations, chooses a different approach and emphasizes the incompatibility between the will or wish to be recognized, and an abstract and merely disrupting, corroding, dissolving negativity. This negativity which is death interrupts the discursive context, at least 'for a time', and consequently cannot fill itself with meaning, with the meaning which turns it into an absolute negativity or into a negativity 'of a positive kind' (Hegel I, 172). The instant death acquires an unambiguous and unified meaning; the instant it starts to make sense; the instant abstract negativity determines itself as absolute negativity, as preserving and surpassing sublation – the discursive context maintains itself as a coherent one and suppresses the possibility of a different experience, of an experience of 'transgression' and 'sovereignty'. Bataille shows that Hegel himself acknowledges such a possibility: 'What nonetheless assures the sovereignty of the moment described is the "absolute dismemberment" of which Hegel speaks, the rupture, for a time, of discourse' (Bataille, 293).

The suppression of a different experience of death is a falsification which reduces the claims based on a 'struggle for life and death', on a daring, endangering and proving, to mere protestations.

After having quoted the lecture on Hegel, Derrida writes in his essay on Bataille: 'It does not suffice to risk death if the putting at stake is not permitted to take off, as chance or accident, but is rather invested as the work of the negative' (Derrida IV, 261). From an objective point of view, Bataille's critique of Hegel and Kojève belongs to the same tradition as Heidegger and Adorno. The following note can be found in the fragments of a treatise on Hegel which Heidegger wrote between 1938 and 1941: 'Negativity is the "energy" of unconditional thought, because from the outset it has given up everything negative, everything that denotes nothingness' (Heidegger VI, 14). Adorno's negative dialectic is, for its part, a 'critique of positive negation' and opens up dialectical experience to the verti-ginous 'shock of the open and inconclusive' (Adorno I, 33).

How exactly do the economy of death of a 'true anthropology' (human beings distinguish themselves from the nothingness of death 'for a certain amount of time') and the economy of death of sovereignty (discourse is interrupted 'for a time') differ from each other? Can one use Derrida's terms here and say that Kojève's notion of an economy of death still serves a 'restricted economy', while Bataille's 'unreserved Hegelianism' removes its limitations, de-limiting and generalizing it?

5. The relationship of recognition is *always* a relationship marked by a certain reciprocity and homogeneity. But the reciprocal and symmetrical relationship between the one who recognizes and the one who is recognized, which is said to constitute the *always* required or demanded meaning of recognition as the double movement of a double self-consciousness, is nowhere more evident than in those paragraphs of the *Encyclopaedia* where Hegel actually equates what results from the struggle for recognition with speculation, with a truth which indicates and reflects itself. The absolutely paradigmatic character of the process of

recognition, the concretion of the unity which in the *Phenomenology* is called a 'unity in the doubling' and which is established by the 'twofold [*doppelsinnig*] sublation' of a 'twofold otherness' that is a 'twofold return into itself' of a double self-consciousness, become apparent at this point:

> Here, then, we have the violent and extraordinary diremption of spirit into different selves which in and for themselves, as well as for each other, are absolutely free and independent, absolutely impenetrable and resistant; and yet, these selves are also identical with each other, they are not independent, not impenetrable, but, as it were, fused with one another. The nature of this relationship is thoroughly *speculative*; and when it is supposed that the speculative is something remote and inconceivable, one has only to consider the content of this relationship to convince oneself of the unfounded character of this opinion. The speculative, or the rational and true, consists in the unity of the concept, or of the subject, and the objectivity. This unity is manifestly present in the standpoint in question.' (Hegel I, 177)

Hegel may well stress that he conceives of the proximity of the speculative in recognition in terms of a simultaneity of identity and non-identity, of release and unified middle. It would hardly be convincing, however, to affirm that the release of the other and the non-identity of the independent self-consciousness with the other self-consciousness are not *ultimately* superseded and preserved within the unity of speculation. Only if they are can the movement of recognition lead on to a result, to the 'fusion' or the merging of those who recognize and those who are recognized. Only if they are can the concept of recognition be formed, the concept on which the possibility of a true discourse must depend, as Kojève re-cognizes. This possibility is the possibility of determining something *as such*, as being this or that.

One can find in Kojève's *Introduction* the following passage:

> Whatever the circumstances may be, human reality can engender itself and preserve its existence only if it is a 'recognized' reality. A human is really human, human for himself and for others, only because he has been 'recognized' by the other, by a number of others and finally by all the others. Only if one speaks of a 'recognized' human reality, can one state a truth in the strict and full sense of the term when calling this reality a human one [therefore, the strict and full sense, the proper meaning of a true discourse, presupposes the truth of recognition as a truth without which there can be no truth, no true statement, no proper meaning, no full sense]. For only in this case is one in a position to reveal a reality through one's own discourse. (Kojève, 16)

Hence Hegel's presentation of the struggle for recognition may have a paradigmatic value for all attempts to describe the movement of recognition. But the paradox it generates is also exemplary, provided a paradox can ever be exemplary. This paradox consists in the fact that, strictly speaking, *there is no such thing as recognition*. It is precisely this paradoxical fact that one can gauge from the dialectic of lordship and bondage. For while desire is not yet a recognition, recognition as a result is no longer a recognition, but a repeated re-cognition, a recognition that always already lets itself be submitted to a repeated re-cognition, or dissolved within it. If one self-consciousness and the other self-consciousness recognize themselves as 'mutually recognizing each other' (Hegel III, 178), then the recognition of the mutual or reciprocal recognition is a repeated re-cognition, since otherwise the struggle for recognition would continue into infinity. One cannot even assume that a movement of recognition exists, given that such an assumption bestows a unified form upon recognition, a unity by means of which recognition must tend towards a result that presupposes what results. In this sense, all politics of recogni*tion* participates in the unification which leads to the systemic unity of absolute idealism; in this sense, all politics of recogni*tion* misses the (radically uncertain) act of recogni*zing*.

IRONY AND RESCUE

In a short story by Grace Paley entitled 'Enormous Changes at the Last Minute', Alexandra, the main character, visits her sick father in a New York hospital. He is disgruntled and shows little understanding of the changes in his daughter's life; he even accuses her of destroying his own life as a result of these changes. 'After that, Alexandra hoped every day for her father's death, so that she could have a child without ruining his interesting life at the very end of it when ruin is absolutely retroactive' (Paley, 133).

The unmistakable irony which permeates the justification of the death wish is the (reflected) irony of fate. When one is still alive and looks back at one's own life, at a life which by virtue of one's having lived on is already marked by a unifying trait, one cannot but wish for one's own death, for a death which preserves the retrospectively established context of life and protects it against a destruction which can occur at the last minute, at the moment of death, and which can threaten life's very unity. One must wish for one's own death because death entails a fateful certainty, and yet also an indefiniteness – one can die at any time. Thus if one decides to pursue the aims of a politics of recognition *as...*, if one demands that an identity, i.e. the unity of a life and a self-consciousness, is politically recognized in order to maintain the unity of a society, a state, a culture, one moves on a conceptual surface which irony has already broken up and which it holds hovering over an unbridgeable abyss. One overlooks the fact that recognition can only be demanded because it stands in a relation of tension to irony, in a relation of tension which allows for no relaxation. One overlooks the fact that, if there is recognition, there is no recognition without irony and no irony without recognition. Irony without recognition is cynicism, recognition without irony is a form of rigorism. Cynicism and rigorism, political corruption and political repression complement each other.

Therefore, the question which must be raised at this point is whether the political impulse of a politics of recognition can be rescued. It will prove difficult to dissociate oneself from the premises of a politics of recognition (*as...*) if one settles for an approach related to the 'theory of the differentiation of modern societies' as developed by Hegel in Jena, and clings to the notion of an 'overall social context' or to a concept of the 'totality of society' (Menke III, 507). If indeed modern societies cannot 'effect the integration' of their members and spheres without 'becoming irreconcilably *split*'; if a society cannot be politically governed as a whole without resorting to terror; if every 'established form of "being recognized" can once again be dissolved [into the conflict-ridden movement of recognition]'; if, in principle, there is no 'integration of society beyond the struggle for supremacy in which its spheres engage'; if the 'differentiated spheres of the ethical and political context of life and of civil society' are not and cannot be linked in such a way that they form a 'positively determined unity' – then the 'dialectic of solidification and liquefaction' remains incompatible not only with a dialectic of reification and communication defined by the logic

203

of discursive communicative action (ibid., 498, n.11), but also with a social '*totality*', and with a dialectically restored symmetry between complementary social spheres which intersect and yet repel each other. To orientate oneself towards such an overall social balance means recapturing that which splits and submitting it to the tendency towards unification. It means that compatibility determines the argumentation.

The *overall* social balance integrates recognition into the totality of society. It does so in the course of the very process of recognizing, and thereby excludes it. If reciprocity and symmetry in recognition were immediately given, if one could immediately find and re-cognize oneself in the other and if the other could immediately find and re-cognize himself in our self-consciousness, recognition would hardly be required. For there to be recognition, the preceding recognition of the other(s) must be an essential requirement of its movement. There is no recognition in a state of pure simultaneity. *One always recognizes the other first.* Recognition is first and foremost an un-conditional recognition of the other. This un-conditionality, which is structural and which resides in the irretrievable precedence of the other, in the finitude without which recognition would be inconceivable, denotes the possibility and the impossibility, the restricting limits of a politics of recognition which aims at instituting reciprocity and symmetry. Recognition answers un-conditionally to an un-conditional demand of the other before it can take into account specific conditions or make something into a condition. The un-conditional demand of the other precedes the movement of recognition and is also embedded in this movement, for otherwise the one who recognizes would not be capable of hearing it and would not be able to recognize the one who demands recognition. The demand is heard and at the same time goes unheard; it is un-conditional, a demand one can barely understand and meet. It causes the hearing to connect and split in a manner unheard of. Recognition comes too late; the other who is to be recognized is already there and has already been recognized, he has already been determined by a recognition, enough to un-conditionally demand recognition: '. . . *we're here . . .*'.

If the structural un-conditionality of the recognizing relationship resides in the demand for recognition, not only in the response to it, then the exposure of the other who makes the demand, an exposure which is itself un-conditional to the extent that recognition establishes that which is to be recognized, puts the one who recognizes in a sovereign position. Whoever hears the un-conditional demand becomes a sovereign because the hearing of the demand creates a distance which separates him from the one who demands recognition. From such a point of view, the one who is to be recognized finds himself in a legally instituted waiting room that is beyond or outside the law, since the un-conditional aspect of a demand which is free from all conditions can be interpreted as corresponding to a state of emergency or exception on which the sovereign individual who recognizes another individual decides. This interpretation is possible because a purely un-conditional demand could not be heard and because the one who recognizes also behaves in a conditioning or determining way. That the un-conditional demand for recognition is conditioned or determined by the one to whom it is addressed, can be gauged from the fact that *the one who makes the demand must have already recognized the one who hears it without knowing anything about him.* Giorgio Agamben shows that modern bio-politics are to be understood as the culminating point of a political history which is structured by sovereignty and hence by the state of emergency or exception, and describes the *zones d'attente*, the waiting-rooms at French international airports as an extension of the concentration camps. They are a topological indicator which provides evidence for the thesis that bio-political supremacy is unbroken and that the sovereign control over bare life continues:

> The stadium in Bari into which the Italian police in 1991 provisionally herded all illegal Albanian immigrants before sending them back to their country, the *Vel d'Hiver* in which the Vichy authorities gathered the Jews before consigning them to the Germans, the concentration camp for foreigners in Cottbus-Sielow in which the Weimar government gathered Jewish refugees from the East, or the *zones d'attente* in French international airports in which foreigners asking to be recognized as refugees are detained, will then equally be camps. In all these cases, an apparently innocuous space (for example, the Arcade hotel in Roissy) actually delimits a space in which the normal order is de facto suspended and in which whether or not atrocities are committed depends not on law but on the civility and ethical sense of the police who temporarily act as sovereign. (Agamben II, 174)

The un-conditionality that lies in the irretrievable precedence of otherness leaves the one who recognizes with no time and no leeway for becoming sovereign and rising above the one who is to be recognized. However, the irony of un-conditionality, the conditional character of the act of hearing which reacts to the demand raised by the other, causes the recognizing relationship to perpetuate sovereignty and even to constitute it. Recognition moves within an undecidability which comprises the undecidability of the state of emergency or exception.

To the extent that recognition is always also an un-conditional recognition of the other, Kierkegaard's elucidation of the relationship between God and man can be discussed in the context of an analysis of the concept of recognition. The relationship between God and man is the topic of the 'Ultimatum' Kierkegaard added to the two extensive treatises which form the second part of *Either/Or*. The one who recognizes proves to be always in the wrong when compared to the one who is to be recognized. He must renounce his claims to recognition and no longer let himself be determined by the will to be recognized by the other if he wants to be able to recognize the other at all; he must expose himself to the other so unconditionally that the very demand for and the very will to mutual recognition can be formed only after the fact: there is not even a reason for renouncing something. Doubtless Kierkegaard's elaboration of the question, concerning the edifying aspect which characterizes the idea that we are always and at all times in the wrong when relating to God, stands in the context of Christian faith and theology. The ultimate intention of the 'Ultimatum' is unmistakable, since the text is a sermon which is introduced by a prayer and which begins with the exegesis of a biblical passage that abounds with allusions to other biblical passages. But it would be short-sighted and untenable to endorse an ill-conceived sociological relativism or an attenuating multiculturalism which plays everything down, making the contextual dependence absolute and reducing the content of the sermon to its determinability within a single context. Of course, this is not to assert that one can simply transfer the reflections of the 'Ultimatum' and inscribe them in a new context, for example in the political and philosophical context of recognition. The shifts involved in such a transferral must not be concealed, just as the possibility of an active interpretation must not be nipped in the bud. Where the concept of recognition is to be discussed, these shifts and changes affect the distinction between an edifying speech and a discourse which does not aim for edification, i.e. the distinction between the finite and the infinite, between the doubt which thwarts the pre-reflective, un-conditional recognition of the other, and the un-conditionality of the relationship to the other. But if this distinction no longer plays a determining role; if religious edification can no longer be shielded from the realm of a deconstructing doubt; and if this impossibility is not to be understood as implicitly establishing the preeminence of spirit, of philosophy, of the conceptual and scientific universality which absolute idealism presupposes and which it strives for – then otherness can no longer be divided into the (conditional) otherness of the other and the (un-conditional) otherness of God, nor indeed into the (conditional) otherness of the political and the (un-conditional) otherness of the ethical. It can no longer be divided into the otherness of the other and the otherness of the Other – provided that in the present this distinction inherits the legacy of the distinction between man and God. In a famous introductory paragraph to the *Phenomenology*, Hegel states the following:

> Whoever seeks mere edification, and whoever wants to shroud in a mist the manifold variety of his earthly existence and of thought, in order to pursue the indeterminate enjoyment of this indeterminate divinity, may look where he likes to find all this. He will find ample opportunity to dream up something for himself and to put on airs. But philosophy must beware of the wish to be edifying. (Hegel III, 6)

How, then, should one attempt an active interpretation of Kierkegaard and outline a general answer to the question of a rescuing of the political impulse which motivates the politics of recognition? The un-conditionality of recognition Kierkegaard discerns in the recognition or the acknowledgement [*erkjendelse*] of God amounts to a conquering of the doubt which dominates finitude; thus it is a movement of the infinite, a relationship of infinity, an infinite relation to the other. The one who recognizes un-conditionally holds no secret wish, he no longer seeks peace in the 'labouring thoughts', in the 'restless mind', in the 'fearful heart', in thinking, desiring and feeling, for they can always be haunted by doubt. To the extent, though, that an unconditional recognition always already rises above all possible doubt, acknowledgement cannot be the result of reflection, of a cognitive act which discloses truth. Re-cognition and repeated re-cognition obtain access to such an acknowledgement only belatedly and hence do not have full access to it. Just as unconditional recognition withdraws from (repeated) re-cognition, and just as the fundamental, indubitable wrong of the one who recognizes cannot be immediately and indubitably clear or intelligible, the un-conditionality of the recognition of the other, which expresses itself in the un-conditional recognition of one's own wrong, resists all forms of rationalization. It is not a consolation or a compensation.

Kierkegaard contrasts the immediate acknowledgement of the infinite(ly) other from a cognitive act, from a previous acknowledgement, from an acknowledgement mediated by cognition. He writes:

> When you acknowledge that God is always in the right, you stand outside God, and likewise when, as a conclusion from that, you acknowledge that you are in the wrong. But when you do not claim and are not convinced by virtue of any previous acknowledgement that you are always in the wrong, then you are hidden in God. (Kierkegaard II, 350)

If one follows the sermon, one understands that one must locate doubt and knowledge in finitude, since both must bridge the gap of belatedness. This gap which threatens to divert knowledge and surrender it to the bad infinity of doubt is brought about by reflection. It belongs to the definition of reflection that it must presuppose the object of its reflection, the object it wants to comprehend in its very truth. Reflection must catch up with something which precedes it, which has already occurred or happened. Absolute determinacy, determinacy without an event, would make the act of reflecting superfluous. Thus reflection has already been affected by something inexplicable before it can reflect upon that which it presupposes in order to grasp and to explain it. When one reflects upon something, the object can prove to be explicable or inexplicable; but the inexplicable also taints the explicable itself, marking all belated explanations and justifications provided in and by the process of reflection:

> Does it explain the unexplainable to say that it has happened only once in the world? Or is this not the unexplainable – that it has happened? And does not this, that it has happened, have the power to make everything else unexplainable, even the explainable? If it happened once in the world that the human condition was essentially different from what it otherwise always is, what assurance is there that it cannot be repeated, what assurance that that was not the true and that what ordinarily occurs is the untrue? Or is it a demonstration of the truth that it happened the most frequently? (ibid., 334)

Something happens and demands to be explained; as a consequence, reflection comes after the fact. Something happens which cannot be explained by means of reflection; reflection is shattered by this impossibility and bears its trace even when it reflects upon something which can be explained. But is the impossibility of fully explaining something not inscribed in the belatedness of all reflection, in the *fact* that reflection must come *after the fact?* Kierkegaard distinguishes the un-conditionality in the recognition or the acknowledgement of the infinite(ly) other, an un-conditionality incompatible with a more-or-less, from the belatedness of recognition, the ubiquity of doubt, the conditionality of the finite. Recognition is un-conditional as experience – as experience of love, for the lover has no time to consider whether or not right is being done to him. His love is determined by one single wish only, as Kierkegaard stresses: the lover wishes 'to be eternally in the wrong'. If he does not want to betray his love, he cannot satisfy himself with the conviction that he is right; he cannot content himself with a calming-down or an appeasement caused by the overcoming of the contradiction. *I never love as the other might love me, I never recognize the other as I might be recognized by him.*

The necessary preservation of the contradiction on which love and recognition depend in their un-conditionality indicates that there is never a purely finite or infinite relationship to the other. One does not rise un-conditionally above the finite to reach the infinite; one does not persist in the conditional and the finite; rather one always brings finitude to the infinite relationship and infinitude to the finite relationship. The recognizing relationship to the other is both conditional and un-conditional: it is conditional because it is a relationship and un-conditional because the otherness of the other must not be repeatedly re-cognizable if it is not to be virtually identical with the selfness of the self who relates to the other. In a sense Kierkegaard himself admits to the impossibility of clearly separating the conditional and the un-conditional when speaking of the 'infinite relationship with a person' (ibid., 348). Love – love for a conditionally and un-conditionally recognized other never has a 'quality of pure inwardness' (Adorno III, 269). The essential diversion of its un-conditionality preserves it from turning into its opposite. But were it to be deprived of its un-conditionality, it would turn into lovelessness.

It is impossible to distinguish unequivocally between an outside and an inside in the recognizing relationship or in the movement of recognition. This means that being in the wrong is not just a privilege, the privilege of a human being who can relate to God; it means that the one who recognizes is not hidden in the other without remaining concealed from himself and the other. Before the one who recognizes can re-cognize the other and himself; before he can repeatedly re-cognize himself in the other, he is concealed from himself when hidden in the other. He is concealed from himself without ever being able to find an identical self, his or the other's; he is hidden without ever being able to assure himself of a still incomplete identity. The fact that the one who recognizes is hidden in the one who is recognized, a fact which is not immune to doubt and which is not protected from the irony which permeates and diverts recognition, does not mean that *something* is safe or that *something* is concealed: what is at stake here is a concealment to which no revelatory discovery of a concealed object can ever correspond. Because one recognizes the other; because recognition is a recognition of the other and the relationship between the one who recognizes and the one who is recognized cannot be objectified; because one cannot identify the one who recognizes and the one who is recognized; because recognition is a *given* only to the extent that it is not *a* given; because there is recognition only to the extent that there *is* no recognition, no conceptual unity of recognition, no stabilized relation of dependency and no integral reciprocity resulting from a struggle for recognition; because even the limitation of recognition in friendship and love to 'relationships involving *adult* love and friendship' (Menke I, 92) curtails the struggle for recognition in advance and thus predetermines it; because irony and doubt can never be brought to rest once and for all, and no one is ever simply right or wrong – one does not re-cognize oneself or the other. One does not re-cognize oneself in the other, and the other does not re-cognize him- or herself in the one who repeatedly re-cognizes his own self in his otherness.

Hence a politics of rescuing responds to a politics of recognition. For one must always rescue that which is not and which *is* only because it is not, that which is not (a) given and which is given only because it is not (a) given. In politics, one is faced with the irony of rescuing, with the rescuing of irony.

APPENDIX: SELFHOOD

Notes on autonomy and recognition*

Nothing is more important than the formation of fictional
concepts, which alone teach us to understand our own.

Ludwig Wittgenstein

Is there a link between autonomy and recognition? If such a link
exists, and if autonomy means to give oneself one's own law,
then two different starting points can be chosen to conceptualize
this link. On the one hand, one can try to justify the assumption
that autonomy cannot constitute itself without recognition. In
this case, recognition proves indispensable to the constitution of
an autonomous subject, whether the subject is conceived of in
terms of an individual consciousness, of self-consciousness in
general, of a collective historical subject, or of a socially mediated
intersubjectivity. In order to attain autonomy, the subject which
constitutes itself in the very movement of attaining autonomy
requires recognition. From this perspective, one would have to
describe the relationship between autonomy and recognition as a

* These notes are based on a lecture that I gave in Prague in 1996 as part of a
course on philosophy and social sciences – A.G.D.

relationship charged with tension, as a tense and tight relationship, as a relationship which keeps one in suspense. For the essential and constitutive dependency on recognition would introduce a heteronomous element, an otherness, into autonomy. On the other hand, however, one can also assume that recognition relates to autonomy as a mere confirmation. If one chooses this premise, one has to ask oneself how the confirming recognition of an already constituted autonomy or of an already formed autonomous subject is to be interpreted. Either one regards the confirmation as something external to autonomy, as something which does not contribute to understanding the formation of the subject to which autonomy is assigned – in which case a link between autonomy and recognition does not exist in any meaningful sense. Or else one regards the confirming recognition as something on which autonomy depends – in which case the relationship between autonomy and recognition is once again placed in the perspective opened up by the first possibility. If a meaningful or relevant link between autonomy and recognition exists, then it must be comprehended as a tension, as a tension which has always already complicated the formation of an autonomous subject and diverted it from its destination.

But why is there a link between autonomy and recognition? Perhaps because one cannot give oneself one's own law without a recognition that one has indeed done this. Such an answer seems convincing if one presupposes that it is no longer possible to maintain a strict separation between acts of freedom and acts subject to the causality of nature. At this point, it is difficult to distinguish between history and structure. The tension which separates autonomy and recognition, yet at the same time relates them to each other, makes it impossible to conceive of the structure of an autonomy which remains essentially dependent on recognition without conceiving of an historical event, of a spatial

and temporal event, of the unnoticed, awaited, surprising, missing, delayed, premature event of recognition. Even a purely formal concept of autonomy depends on such an event. Those who
work in the area of social philosophy and defend a purely formal
concept of autonomy seek to protect this concept from the
undesired effects of a constitutive recognition, to protect form
from deformation. Therefore they posit a universal autonomy
which encompasses the whole of society and which is revoked
only when the individual or the subject to whom autonomy has
been assigned attracts attention because of his 'abnormal' behaviour. Yet the admission of possible exceptional cases forces these
defenders of a purely formal concept of autonomy to ask themselves whether it is not the case that all forms of autonomy
depend on a recognition they are incapable of controlling. Such
a dependency can sometimes be very obvious, sometimes less so.
The exceptional case may reveal and also shatter the normalizing
and stabilizing function of a recognition which is already presupposed by a purely formal and universal autonomy; when faced
with an exceptional case, the formalism may suddenly appear as
a concealment which ensures that the exception and the tension
between autonomy and recognition become invisible in all so-
called normal cases.

If, like recognition, autonomy cannot attain the stability of a
result; if it cannot do so because of the tension which traverses
its relation to a constitutive recognition, then it does not characterize a unified subject or a unified intersubjectivity, both instances of thought which are identical with themselves and which
can be identified as being identical. Perhaps it is helpful here to
refer to the self-referential movement that Adorno, in a rarely
noticed and rather enigmatic passage of his *Aesthetic Theory*, calls
selfhood. This concept is applied to an object of artistic contemplation, at least in the immediate context in which it occurs.

However, the second example of selfhood given by Adorno points to the possibility of expanding the usage of the concept:

> As for those vases, it seems that they are similar to language in that they suggest something which means 'Here I am' or 'This is me', something which touches on a selfhood identifying thought has not yet isolated from the interdependency of beings. In the same way, a rhinoceros, this speechless animal, appears to say 'I am a rhinoceros.' (Adorno VI, 112)

A selfhood in Adorno's sense is not an individual or a collective subject; it is not an intersubjective subjectivity; it is not a subject or a subjectivity which identifies itself as such and thus reveals itself to be autonomous. If anything can be said about it at all, it is probably that it must be understood as a pure self-reference or as a pure expression. A selfhood does not posit itself as a selfhood; it does not constitute itself in an act of self-identification; it does not dispose of an identity and cannot be identified as a selfhood. It does not simply stand in the 'interdependency of beings'; yet it does not leave it behind either, as if it were an identifiable selfhood. It does not give itself its own law and is still nothing but its own expression, a pure expression which consists in a gesture similar to language, in a self-indication. This indication should not be confused with a statement. A selfhood neither dissolves into the abstract generality of the generic nor persists in the abstract singularity of an *individuum ineffabile*. It is almost impossible to think of a self-positing, a self-affirmation and a self-identification without the self-reference of a selfhood. However, this reference exceeds the posited solidity of a subject identical with itself; it corresponds to the excess of an autonomy for which recognition is constitutive, an excess neither autonomous nor heteronomous. If the act of recognizing is traversed by the tension which exists between an establishment and a confirmation, then selfhood seems to inaugurate and to perpetuate the struggle for recognition, given that on the one hand it is a confirmation, a 'Here I am' or 'This is me', while on the other hand stating nothing: it behaves as if it demanded an establishing recognition. But within the struggle for recognition in which, as has been suggested, the constitution of autonomy becomes involved, the selfhood remains a threshold one can never cross once and for all. The question regarding the link or the relationship between autonomy and recognition is the question regarding the threshold of a selfhood.

'Trying to live in such a way that I can believe myself to have been a good animal' – the famous sentence with which Adorno concludes his 'Metacritique of Practical Reason' in *Negative Dialectics* (Adorno I, 299), refers to that threshold-existence for which he uses the concept or the name selfhood. In selfhood as threshold ethics and aesthetics converge. It is the place and the expression of a pure and exposed 'There/this is me.'

NOT ALWAYS BEING GOOD

Appendix to the English translation

At one point in her incisive commentary on multiculturalism, Silvia Bovenschen writes of a peculiar relief. A person who is open to the foreign and friendly to foreigners may on occasion admit that he cannot stand a certain people. Bovenschen does not trace this admission back to a prejudice, to a pattern of behaviour typical of the authoritarian character, but rather to the attempt 'to unburden oneself a little of eternally being good and right' (Bovenschen III, 298).

It is doubtless possible to explain this attempted unburdening by asserting that it reflects a quasi-compulsive behaviour. The temptation to deviate from what one is expected to believe and do, is most irresistible when nothing seems to suggest such a challenge. An inconspicuous change proves then to be sufficient to create a distance from what is expected, to experience the expected as an unbearable burden, and to betray it in the name of an abstract possibility. Thus, for example, the ethos of a speaker, or the idea that he and his audience have of what is good, imply that he makes an effort to be good at what he does, that he tries to be inventive. But the speaker who anticipates such an expectation and writes his paper under its burden may be tempted by the possibility of not letting himself be guided by the expected 'being good', and of not seeking to be right in the end, at least for once. What will he come up with, what will catch his attention? A cousin of the one who deviates from an expectation for the sake of a possibly liberating possibility, is the judge who figures in Gary Indiana's novel *Resentment*. During a trial in Los Angeles, 'his fingers are busy lining up exactly so the staples and paper clips attached to various documents on his blotter: sometimes, when these little bits of metal run askew, the risk of an 8.3 earthquake [. . .] becomes dramatically present' (Indiana, 297).

However, such an explanation of the behaviour Bovenschen alludes to is insufficient to the extent that it does not account for what is at stake in 'being good' or 'being right'. One can, of course, choose a different approach to explain this strange behaviour, this experiment with an uncertain outcome. One can try to justify the attempt at unburdening oneself by interpreting the challenging recourse to an idiosyncrasy which has not yet turned into a prejudice as a dismantling or an unmasking. In this case, a general consensus is supposed to be unmasked, a conformism through which 'being good' and 'being right' have become ossified, functioning as mere identification badges which denote a belonging, or as elements of a ritual. This ritual serves the purpose of mutual confirmation and hence of excluding what is foreign. It leads to a dogmatic rigidification which tolerates no deviations, no critical questions, nothing foreign, disturbing or alienating. Yet such an interpretation amounts to a comforting playing down of the issue if it is itself informed by a 'being good' or a 'being right' and does not perceive an expression of shame in the unmasking and dismantling. It is presented, then, in order once again to avoid a critical question, the question of whether it is possible to be good and at the same time be aware of being good, of following recognized norms, of corresponding to justified expectations. Can one be aware of one's own being good and be right with respect to the one who should be good but is not because he has not yet attained an undistorted awareness or consciousness of his thinking and acting?

This question will now be explored in an analysis of the ideas Christoph Menke develops in his book *Tragedy in Ethical Life*. The book ends with a 'preview' of 'the good' [*das Gute*], with a 'view' unlocked by 'the good'. The notion of the good which appears in this 'view' or which promises such a 'view', must be distinguished from other notions of the good which it is meant to comprise within itself and which, for this reason, already unlock the view onto the good of which they partake. In the very isolation, limitation and blindness of their complementary and yet incompatible comprehension of the good, these other notions are part of a larger notion of the good which overcomes their incompatibility and transforms their blindness into an insight. The moment the individual has forever left behind the substantiality of ethical life in which he has no consciousness of what is good because spirit, as Hegel writes, appears to be an 'immediate truth' and has not proceeded to gain a 'consciousness of what it actually is in such immediacy' (Hegel III, 326); the moment the individual has entered a 'legal condition' in which his 'living individuality' is separated from everything he 'shares politically' with other individuals, the good splits up. Menke distinguishes between the idea of an equality which embraces all individuals and every single one of them, from the idea of the 'authenticity' of a particular existence which orients itself towards its 'self-realization'. A 'public justice' is said to watch over equality, while a 'singular justice' is said to preserve and restore the integrity and integrality of an authentic existence.

Menke does not explicitly discuss a splitting-up of the good into distinct notions or ideas of the good. The principle of equality which is guarded by 'public justice' and whose intactness, as will

be shown, ultimately depends on the intended success of a 'reciprocal recognition' should not be subsumed under the concept
of the good, given that individuality belongs to the '"semantic"
determination' of this concept; for Menke, the good is primor-
dially 'individual'. It is always one's own good, the good of a
singular individual defined in terms of his peculiarities and
idiosyncrasies. However, Menke does concede that the specific
content of the good can always be formed by the 'shared good',
by the 'values and goods of the social order'; he even says that
the 'individually good' can be determined only with regard to
the 'shared good' (Menke IV, 197). One can speak of a splitting-
up of the good for two reasons. On the one hand, the idea of
equality in the 'legal condition' must doubtless belong to what is
'politically shared' and cannot really be separated from the 'shared
good', for otherwise the realm of legality and the realm of the
life-world would be opposed to each other in an abstract fashion.
Against such an abstract opposition, one can refer to the fact
that an individual is 'recognized' as a person in the legal realm,
as well as to the possibility of violating the principle of equality
by means of the idea of what is 'individually good'. On the other
hand, though, Menke's notion of a unified good which unites
legal equality and the 'individually good', prospectively and retrospectively justifies the discussion of a splitting or a doubling of
the good.

The good splits up into two or three manifestations of itself,
into a 'politically shared' form of equality, into the 'shared good'
of the life-world, and into the 'individually good' which, located
in the life-world, either accepts, overcomes or transgresses the
'shared good'. But how is the 'shared good' defined in the 'legal
condition', if the good can be defined only individually and if
only the moral, political and legal principle of equality which all
individuals share, once an abstraction from their individuality

has taken place, can be defined in a way which is not primarily individual? Is the 'shared good' – which the 'individually good' is supposed to require for it to be defined – a rudiment of ethical life?

'Public justice' aims for the maintenance and restoration of equality in law, 'singular justice' for the maintenance and restoration of individual well-being. Menke sets self-determination, the autonomy of the person or of the legally equal agent, in opposition to self-realization, to the fulfilled and good life of the unequal individual:

> Self-realization is not and does not imply self-determination. Rather, self-determination is what must be legally presupposed in order to guarantee that the consequences of the preeminence of law are not perceived as repressive, as a sign of domination, and must not be deplored. (ibid., 297)

Self-determination defines primarily the person, self-realization determines primarily the individual. Yet if the autonomy of the subject is to ensure that as a person, as a legally equal agent, the individual does not experience the constraining demands which law addresses to him, as foreign and purely external impositions, then self-determination must always imply the self-realization it makes possible; Menke affirms that 'public justice' refers to those 'general conditions' which are required 'for the establishment of the individually good' (ibid., 225). Were these conditions to be brought about arbitrarily and were they therefore to be arbitrary in themselves; were they to be 'particular conditions', then the 'establishment of the individually good' would itself be exposed to arbitrariness, to an arbitrary revocability which would mark its constitution. The 'establishment of the individually good' would be a privilege, the 'individually good' would be something evil, at least virtually. Aware of one's privilege, one would cling to it stubbornly and obstinately, or desperately lost, filled with the blind trust of one who has been elected or who has a mission. Such trust could then turn into a blinding self-righteousness which would never cease to provoke doubts. Conversely, the self-realization which establishes the ideal of the 'individually good' and orients itself towards it implies a self-determination: not only because it would remain an impotent endeavour without the 'general conditions' which secure its possibility, but also because only an autonomous, free and self-determining subject can consciously realize itself. Self-determination implies self-realization, while self-realization implies the free determination of a self which determines itself. However, the person and the individual do not simply coincide. Self-determination and self-realization therefore also diverge from each other and relate to each other differently in a person and in an individual.

The awareness or the consciousness of the good comes about the moment the good splits up, triggering a necessarily partial experience of the heterogeneity which distinguishes the homogeneity of the public sphere from the heterogeneity of individual peculiarities and singularities. Thus the consciousness of the good is itself a divided consciousness. Its division, though, already discloses a 'view' onto a restored unity, onto the wholly and really good. According to Menke, the unity of the good, the wholly and really good, is established by a 'sovereign subject', by a subject which is sovereign because it sets itself free in its very preservation and preserves itself in its very freedom. This subject endures its division, its splitting up into a person and an individual, into a subject which is free enough to create, maintain and reestablish legal equality, and into a subject which is free enough to constitute itself individually and to realize itself to lasting effect. The 'sovereign' subject is capable of distancing itself reflectively from the heterogeneity which marks the good; it can transform the being-not-one of the good into a being-one. It is capable of exceeding the autonomy of the person and the self-realization of individuality because it is able to present to them the conflict which sets them in opposition to each other. Moving beyond the conflict between a person and an individual, the 'sovereign' subject 'completes' itself; it unfolds the full 're-flective power' and the full 'freedom' of subjectivity. This subject is free to the extent that it can abandon itself without getting lost; it is reflective to the extent that, having delivered itself to the one-sidedness of the two limited and limiting figures of the good, it always keeps an eye on the unlimited good which appears in an obstructed or restricted 'view' – in a 'view' of and onto the wholly and really good.

The 'sovereign' subject can restore the unity of the good be-cause its possibility is contained in the good which has split away from itself and which becomes manifest in the form of a 'view' or a 'preview'. What is at stake here is the 'possibility of the good' and of a 'sovereign subject' without which the 'view' would remain entirely obstructed. Nevertheless, the 'sovereign' subject does not simply restore the unity of the good. It rather estab-lishes this unity for the first time; it discloses for the first time the 'view' of and onto the good, since the restored unity differs from the one of the irrevocably lost ethical life. It must be con-sidered as a precarious awareness or consciousness of the good, as the *unity of a consciousness of a unified good*, i.e. as the unity of a *self-consciousness*. The 'view' of and onto the good is a 'view' of and onto an achieved and completed subjectivity. In the unified good, the good and subjectivity retrieve their presupposition and assert themselves for the first time as something achieved and complete, even if nothing guarantees that the realization of the good is possible in principle. In the wholly and really good, in

225

the completely subjective, the 'view' is already a 'view' which is disclosed by what the 'view' discloses. In other words, once the wholly and really good is attained, once subjectivity has completed itself, a 'view' no longer exists. Something is promising or hopeless; something offers an attractive view or no view at all only in the interval between the division and the unification of the good, the diremption and the completion of subjectivity. In the last paragraph of his book, Menke maintains that

> we are not hopelessly caught up in the collisions of law and well-being, despite their tragic necessity. For there is always the possibility of the good: the possibility of an integration of law and well-being by means of the sovereign freedom of the subject. (ibid., 315f.)

What Menke says about the tragic character and the necessity of conflicts in his impressive, inventive and precise reconstruction of Hegel's 'tragedy in ethical life' can be applied to the conflictual relationship which links and interrupts his concepts of subjectivity, of justice and of the good. If what is called tragic amounts to 'the "necessary" coming into conflict of that which is itself "necessary"' (ibid., 29); if the dissolution of a substantial ethical life inevitably leads to the emergence of a split subjectivity, a split justice and a split good; if the conflict, the collision, the clash of that which splits results from its own description and precedes its actual 'coming into conflict' (ibid., 33) with itself – then we are faced with the following contradiction. On the one hand, no legal realm of equality can be delimited in which justice would be concerned with the 'authenticity' of the individual, with his own good. On the other hand, no such realm can constitute itself without a 'transformation of justice' (ibid., 77) which generates a 'singular justice'. Subjectivity, justice and the good each refer to themselves, but they are also split within themselves. Therefore, their concepts do not denote an already existing conceptual unity. Rather, they denote a movement, or a process which is teleological because it is guided by the 'view' of a prospective unification. This process is designed to establish and restore conceptual unity. But does the good ever come into 'view'; does it ever offer a 'view', a 'view' onto itself as a conscious good, if it proves to be impossible to be good and at the same time conscious of being good? I follow a maxim, a norm, an imperative; I distinguish and decide according to the stipulations of a value, of a set of values; I make an effort to do the right thing and to correspond to an idea or a representation of the good: to the idea of equality (all individuals and each one of them are equal), *and* to the idea of the good (I am concerned with the good as an individual who belongs to a religious or a secular community, who has a particular character, who relates to life in an experimental or aesthetic way). Ultimately, I seek to do justice to the idea of the good which unites both the idea of the individually good, of the good linked to the peculiarity of an individual, and the consciousness of the moral, political and legal principle of equality. In doing so, I orient myself towards the normative and evaluative aspect of the good. Be good, behave such that your life can be judged to be good. It can be judged to be good because 'public justice' which presupposes the principle of equality has created conditions for living a good life and because you can find yourself in what is good for you. I look up to the good and expose myself to its gaze. Am I good in this case, as good as I can possibly be?

The fact that a person, a legally equal individual, does not dispose of a fixed identity, and that, for this reason, self-determination in the sphere of law is limited, or constitutively open to something unavailable and mobile; the fact that 'public justice' is also a form of 'singular justice', a relationship to a generalized individuality in which it must not exhaust itself, constitutively open and mobile because incapable of relating to a permanently established identity of the person; the fact that the principle of equality acquires its constitutive mobility and openness because of what remains unavailable and blinding in the concept of a person and of 'public justice', means that the 'legal condition' is not a 'secured condition' and that it is marked by a movement filled with tension, by a 'processuality' (ibid., 226) to which Menke alerts the reader repeatedly. This 'processuality' divides the concept of the person, the concept of 'public justice' and the concept of the good which lies in the principle of equality. It divides concepts which result from a division, from the division of the concept of the subject, of the concept of justice, of the concept of the good; in a word: of the concept of the good as a concept of a just self-consciousness. The '"necessary" coming into conflict of that which is itself "necessary"' must affect what comes into conflict, must trigger a conflict in that which comes into conflict. Otherwise the conflict would remain external to what comes into conflict and could not be described as a necessary conflict. The 'processuality' takes place between one subject and the other, between one justice and the other, between one form of the good and the other, and also within one subject and the other, within one justice and the other, within one form of the good and the other. However, it is an 'immanent' (ibid., 226) processuality, a processuality inherent in the 'legal condition' only to the extent that it can be comprehended teleologically, as a processuality which lets itself be guided by the 'view' that a sovereign subjectivity or the wholly and really good discloses: by a 'view' onto a finally succeeding 'integration' which puts an end to a conflict that reproduces itself irremediably and 'incessantly'. The relevance of the concept of recognition for

Menke's account of justice and freedom becomes evident now, even if the usage Menke makes of it is never explicitly justified by an analysis or an investigation of the concept itself. Menke must attribute to recognition an essential significance when discussing the possibility of exercising 'public justice', since without it, without a recognition of a person as a person, of the equality of all individuals as an equality of each one of them, 'public justice' would fall prey to a one-sided abstraction. It would fall prey to a 'loss of reality' (ibid., 209) and the conflict between the two forms or figures of justice would endlessly repeat itself in the midst of the hopelessness of a bad infinity and its obstructed view. The abstraction of equality must be a double abstraction, it must allow for the consideration of all individuals, but also for the consideration of each one of them. It must create and recognize a space with enough leeway for 'an event of continuous recognition' to occur. It must bring about the autonomy of the subject and at the same time ground itself in the subjective 'faculty' of 'repeating the processes of abstraction which are constitutive of law' and of becoming 'the author of (a process of) recognition' (ibid., 232 and 228). For a reconciliation between 'public' and 'singular' justice to come into 'view'; for the establishment of the wholly and really good to appear as a prospect, the subject resulting from the abstraction which lets a person emerge must be certain of having been recognized, and 'singular justice' must not simply be opposed to the abstraction which is the condition for 'public justice' to be exercised. Menke consistently conceptualizes law as a 'happening in the course of which justice is exercised in such a way that all persons are recognized' (ibid., 215); he does not conceptualize it as a mere state of affairs. But if the concept of a person is inscribed in such a happening, in 'an event of continuous recognition', then it can never be used as if it were given once and for all. The concept of a person belongs to those 'concealed presuppositions of homogenization' of a state of affairs which only a happening can bring to light. It is derived from a double abstraction which starts out with 'the "concrete" determinations of the "different" individuals', as Menke puts it in his paper on the 'self-reflection of morality' (Menke V, 14), and ends up with abstracting from the abstraction by concealing the abstraction itself. Thus the concept of a person is and must be subjected to constant revision, to a revision which disturbs the immobility of our thoughts and unhinges the certainty of the immobility of their object. As a revision of a presupposed concept of a person, as a dissolving of a state of affairs by means of a happening or a process which expands a particular and limited 'legal universality', the movement of recognition is regulated by an understanding of the other. This understanding is never more unconstrained and comprehensive; it never sees the world with as many eyes as in the transcending and reflective presentation with which a 'sovereign' subjectivity recognizes and cognitively grasps the collision between a person and an individual. Because it refers to a 'process of reciprocal recognition' which it keeps going, and not to a 'state of "being recognized"', an understanding 'public justice' offers a 'view' onto a possible reconciliation of that which has split off and does not appear as the incomprehensible judgement of an 'external fate' (Menke IV, 227), as an event which arbitrarily and violently befalls the individual.

The good of individuality and the principle or the idea of equality have in common that they must be established, instituted, produced. Three possibilities of becoming aware of the individually good, or of gaining a notion of it, disclose the 'view' (ibid., 199) onto 'one's own good'. 'One's own good', the good peculiar to own's own individuality, is never 'simply and immediately there', but once it is 'there', once the individual has finally found, invented, appropriated, posited it, its destruction is said to destroy the individual himself. Hence freedom and bondage of the individual reside in the good which it makes into its 'own good'. The 'individually good' becomes the individual's innermost fate, regardless of whether the individual defines himself by means of an 'affirmative adoption', an 'irreversible overcoming' or a 'constant transgression' of the 'shared good'. The realization of one of these three possibilities of gaining a notion of the 'individually good' becomes the individual's innermost fate, his unavoidable destiny, because each possibility indicates an identifiable and excluding determination, a channelling which points the way ahead, a limitation Menke calls 'ethical', a condensation and a correction of the reflecting 'aesthetic' force which must be set free for a realization – a self-realization – to be conceivable in the first place.

Of the 'five forms' of an 'authentic life' which the individual appropriates by means of an adoption, an overcoming or a transgression of the 'shared good', the form of the 'experiment' deserves special attention. For it is not just an additional possibility in a series of given possibilities, a possibility which supplements other possibilities and widens the range of existent possibilities. It is already contained in all the other possibilities and precedes their series as a sort of originary possibility. In a 'legal condition' in which no attachment to a life-world and to 'one's own good' can remain immune to the force of abstraction which dissolves the substantial nature of ethical life and what is particular to oneself, the attachment to the sacral, to a community, or to one's character, always implies a threatening 'radicalization'. Nothing protects the search for an 'authentic life' and the 'individually good' from its transformation into an experimental behaviour; on the contrary, it already tends towards such behaviour. Thus, one cannot but generalize the insight which may serve to justify the experiment as a form of life: 'Because no one can ever be certain of having found what is particular to him or her, an authentic life consists precisely in carrying out this experimental search or quest' (ibid., 283).

The fifth form of life Menke enumerates is the 'aesthetic' disposition. It is meant to be different from the fourth form of life, from a 'life as experiment', because it is not oriented towards experimenting, towards the success which must measure itself against the uninterrupted continuation of the experiment, but towards a 'specifically aesthetic idea of succeeding' which determines its authenticity (ibid., 288, 293). Yet to the extent that such succeeding must relate to the positing of forms and to their intuition, it is menaced by a de-arting, by what Adorno terms *Entkunstung*. To no less a degree than the substantial nature of ethical life and what is particular to oneself, it is threatened by an abstraction whose force and violence can be experienced in the domain of law, even if the 'legal condition' tries to confine this force and this violence, surrounding it with uncertain limits. The radicalization which transforms a life into an experimental life is inherent in a search whose horizon is formed by the 'specifically aesthetic idea of succeeding' just as much as it is inherent in a search which seeks to find the substantial nature of ethical life or of what is particular to oneself.

What consequences can be drawn from the fact that an experimental form of life stands both inside *and* outside of the series of forms of life Menke analyses? One of the most far-reaching consequences of this peculiar double position of the experimental disposition consists in its making the delimitation of identifiable and mutually exclusive determinations permeable. The experiment is more and something other than a form of life which can be described within its limits, or than an individual search which is guided by a specific and specifiable idea of the 'individually good'. Thus one occasionally encounters disturbing and perhaps even disturbed human beings who are courteous but who do not appear to participate in a quest for the good, a quest for an authentic form of life in which they could realize themselves. One encounters them for example in literature: think of Bartleby. A force or a power of abstraction which has already been objectified when a discourse distinguishes and defines a form of life and what is 'individually good', is at work in the experimental disposition, in the experiment as a form of life. For this reason, the conflict between colliding forms or figures of justice presented by Menke is haunted by another conflict which cannot be grasped and which resists its presentation and its rep-resentation. The conflict Menke presents is a conflict between objectified forces, between an abstraction objectified in the idea of equality and in the intended succeeding of a 'reciprocal recognition', and an abstraction objectified in the 'individually good' and its corresponding form of life. The conflict which haunts this conflict is the conflict between abstraction and its objectifications – objectifications which are supposed to protect the subject and justice from being struck blind.

To the extent that Menke's presentation of 'tragedy in ethical life' is oriented towards the representation or the idea of the good, it is located within the homogeneity created by objecti-fication. Because the colliding forces are objectified forces which can be identified and named; because they are effective within a delimited field of view, albeit one of infinite approximation to the idea of equality and to the realization of what is 'one's own good', only a hesitation betrays the fact that the represented conflict is haunted by the conflict between abstraction and its representations: a hesitation between unification and opening, between a state of being recognized which is anticipated by the idea of equality and a movement of recognition which is never

233

appeased, between a possibility which cannot be realized and a possible realization, between a widening, integrating presentation and a 'freedom from all that is represented'. The conflict between abstraction and its representations cannot be objectified and represented by a 'sovereign' subjectivity. Its unlimited sphere of power encompasses the distance one may wish to gain in order to objectify and represent it.

Perhaps one cannot do without an idea of the 'shared' and the 'individually' good, without an idea of equality and 'reciprocal recognition'. Yet when the good is supposed to disclose a 'view' which justifies our referring to it; when, aware of the good, we make a real effort and try to do the right thing; when, representing the good, we believe that we are approaching it – the good of what is 'politically shared', the 'shared' good of the life-world and the 'individually' good – we cannot but miss it. Why? Because we must deny the unavailability which interrupts the relationship between the good and consciousness, between the good and representation, between the good and presentation. We deny the anarchy which has the effect of a lack and an absence: the good is not given and available. That one has to look for it and find out whether one has actually found it, never being certain of one's success and of the success of recognition, manifests the lack and the absence of the good in its very objectification.

Maybe the good is a passion, the self-forgetfulness of an active pursuit which does not look for a justification out of the corner of its eyes, since it does not result from a choice, from weighing the advantages and disadvantages, and since it does not account to itself or to others for what it does or does not do. Along with Meister Eckhart, one could say that the good belongs to the active life which is close to things in the world, thereby distinguishing itself from a contemplative life which triggers the suspicion of persisting in contemplation only to better enjoy a 'cosy feeling'. Along with Lévinas, one could say that the good is a beyondness that emerges at the farthest extremity of being where substitution, the being-for-the-other, has left behind all calculation and all balancing compensation. In a story by Ginevra Bompiani, we read the following:

> Passion makes no choice, it falls into the depths of the well. Whoever is free to choose, has not been gripped by a passion. This is why one cannot ask a passion to justify its actions. One must interpret each one as changes in the sky and on earth. Passion cannot offer anything as an excuse. Head down and with its eyes lowered, it blindly moves its bulk forward. (Bompiani, 134)

ABOUT THIS BOOK

In May 1994 I held a lecture at the Nordrhein-Westfälisches Kulturinstitut which was subsequently published in an issue of the journal *Babylon* under the title 'We're queer, we're here, so get fuckin' used to it' (nos. 13–14, 1994). Some of the ideas I attempt to develop in *Between Cultures* were first expressed in this lecture. I would like to thank above all Jacques Derrida and Eckart Förster for their suggestions and the opportunity to engage with them in amicable conversation in Paris and San Francisco. My friend Kenneth Woodgate has provided the reader with the best possible translation of this book. I am most grateful to him. *Between Cultures* is a conceptual book, a book about the concept of recognition and about the limits encountered by the formation of concepts.

A.G.D.
London, December 1996/January 1999

BIBLIOGRAPHY

Theodor W. Adorno
I   *Negative Dialectics*, tr. E.B. Ashton, New York: Seabury 1973.
II 'Auferstehung der Kultur in Deutschland?', in Th.W.A., *Kritik*, Frankfurt/M.: Suhrkamp 1973.
III 'Kierkegaards Lehre von der Liebe', in Th.W.A., *Kierkegaard. Konstruktion des Ästhetischen*, Frankfurt/M.: Suhrkamp 1963.
IV *Minima Moralia: Reflections from Damaged Life*, tr. E.F.N. Jephcott, London: NLB 1974.
V   'Trying to Understand *Endgame*', in Th.W.A., *Notes to Literature*, tr. S.W.N. Nicholson, New York: Columbia U.P. 1991.
VI *Aesthetic Theory*, tr. R. Hullot-Kentor, London: Athlone 1997.

Giorgio Agamben
I   *Quel che resta di Auschwitz. L'archivio e il testimone*, Torino: Bollati Boringhieri 1998.
II *Homo Sacer. Sovereign Power and Bare Life*, Stanford/Calif.: Stanford U.P. 1998.

Karl Otto Apel
'Kontingente Identität und historische Haftung', in *Babylon*, no. 7, Frankfurt/M. 1990.

BIBLIOGRAPHY

J.L. Austin
How to Do Things with Words, Oxford: Clarendon 1975.

Alain Badiou
L'éthique. Essai sur la conscience du Mal, Paris: Hatier 1993.

Roland Barthes
Empire of Signs, tr. R. Howard, London: Jonathan Cape 1982.

Georges Bataille
'Hegel, Death and Sacrifice', in G.B., *The Bataille Reader*, ed. F. Botting and S. Wilson, Oxford: Blackwell 1997.

Samuel Beckett
The Theatrical Notebooks of Samuel Beckett, vol. 2, *Endgame*, with a revised text, ed. S.E. Gontarski, London: Faber 1992.

Leo Bersani
Homos, Cambridge/Mass.: Harvard U.P. 1995.

Ginevra Bompiani
L'incantato, Milano: Garzanti 1987.

Christophe Bourdin
Le fil, Paris: Editions de la Différence 1994.

Silvia Bovenschen
I   'Die Bewegungen der Freundschaft', in *Neue Rundschau* 1986, no. 4, Frankfurt/M.
II   'Lob der Nuance. Zur Rettung des Exzentrischen', in *Kursbuch*, December 1994, Berlin.
III   *Schlimmer machen, schlimmer lachen. Aufsätze und Streitschriften*, Frankfurt/M.: Verlag der Autoren 1998.

Judith Butler
Subjects of Desire: Hegelian Reflections in Twentieth-Century France, New York: Columbia U.P. 1987.

John Cage
Silence: Lectures and Writings, Middletown/Conn.: Wesleyan U.P. 1961.

Stanley Cavell
'Knowing and Acknowledging', in S.C., *Must We Mean What We Say?*, Cambridge: Cambridge U.P. 1976.

Gilles Deleuze (with Claire Parnet)
Dialogues, tr. H. Tomlinson and B. Habberjam, London: Athlone 1987.

Jacques Derrida
I   *Mémoires: for Paul de Man*, revised edition, tr. C. Lindsay, New York: Columbia U.P. 1989.
IIa   *Limited Inc.*, Evanston/Ill.: Northwestern U.P. 1987.
IIb   *Limited Inc.*, Paris: Galilée 1990.
III   'Qual Quelle', in J.D., *Margins of Philosophy*, tr. A. Bass, Chicago/Ill.: University of Chicago Press 1982.
IV   'From Restricted to General Economy. A Hegelianism without reserve', in J.D., *Writing and Difference*, tr. A. Bass, London: Routledge & Kegan Paul 1978.

Ronald Dworkin
Life's Dominion. An Argument about Abortion, Euthanasia and Individual Freedom, New York: Knopf 1993.

Frantz Fanon
Black Skin, White Masks, tr. C.L. Markmann, New York: Grove 1967.

Shoshana Felman
I   *Testimony* (with Dori Laub), New York: Routledge 1992.
II   *The Literary Speech Act*, Ithaca/N.Y.: Cornell U.P. 1983.

Eckhart Förster
'I Regard Reason as the Beginning of the Understanding', in E.F., *Kant's Final Synthesis*, Cambridge/Mass.: Harvard U.P. (forthcoming in 2000).

Michel Foucault
'My body, this paper, this fire', in *Oxford Literary Review*, no. 4, 1979.

Gottlob Frege
I   'Negation', in G.F., *Logical Investigations*, tr. P.T. Geach and R.H. Stoothoff: New Haven/Conn.: Yale U.P. 1977.
II 'Thoughts', in G.F., *Logical Investigations*, tr. P.T. Geach and R.H. Stoothoff: New Haven/Conn.: Yale U.P. 1977.

Sigmund Freud
I   *Civilization and its Discontents*, in *The Standard Edition of the Complete Psychological Works of Sigmund Freud*, ed. J. Strachey, vol. 21, London: Hogarth 1961.
II *Beyond the Pleasure Principle*, in *The Standard Edition of the Complete Psychological Works of Sigmund Freud*, ed. J. Strachey, vol. 18, London: Hogarth 1955.
III 'Negation', in *The Standard Edition of the Complete Psychological Works of Sigmund Freud*, ed. J. Strachey, vol. 19, London: Hogarth 1961.

Hans-Jost Frey
Interruptions, tr. G. Albert, Albany: State University of New York Press 1996.

Hans-Georg Gadamer
I   *Truth and Method*, tr. J. Weinsheimer and D.G. Marshall, 2nd edn, London: Sheed & Ward 1989.
II 'Hegel's Dialectic of Self-consciousness', in H.-G.G., *Hegel's Dialectic. Five Hermeneutical Studies*, tr. P.C. Smith, New Haven/Conn.: Yale U.P. 1971.

Jean Genet
L'ennemi déclaré, Paris: Gallimard 1991.

Jürgen Habermas
I   *The Philosophical Discourse of Modernity: Twelve Lectures*, tr. F. Law-
     rence, Cambridge: Polity 1987.
II   'Struggles for Recognition in Constitutional States', in *European
     Journal of Philosophy*, vol. 1, no. 2, August 1993.
III *Between Facts and Norms: Contributions to a Discourse Theory of
     Law and Democracy*, tr. W. Rehg, Cambridge: Polity 1996.

Werner Hamacher
'One 2 Many Multiculturalisms', in *Violence, Identity and Self-Determi-
nation*, ed. Hent de Vries and Samuel Weber, Stanford/Calif.:
Stanford U.P. 1997.

G.W.F. Hegel
I   *Hegel's Philosophy of Mind*, tr. W. Wallace and A.V. Miller,
     Oxford: Clarendon 1971.
II   *Aesthetics. Lectures on fine Art*, tr. T.M. Knox, Oxford: Clarendon
     1975.
III *Phenomenology of Mind*, tr. A.V. Miller, Oxford: Oxford U.P. 1977.
IV   *Jenaer Realphilosophie*, Hamburg: Meiner 1969.

Martin Heidegger
I   *Identity and Difference*, tr. J. Stambaugh, New York: Harper &
     Row 1969.
II   *The Principle of Reason*, tr. R. Lilly, Bloomington: Indiana U.P.
     1991.
III *Die Metaphysik des deutschen Idealismus (Schelling)*, in M.H.,
     Gesamtausgabe, vol. 49, Frankfurt/M.: Klostermann 1991.
IV   'On the Essence of Truth', in *Basic Writings*, ed. D.F. Krell, New
     York: Harper & Row 1977.

V *Nietzsche*, vol. 1, tr. D.F. Krell, San Francisco: Harper & Row 1979.
VI *Hegel*, in M.H., *Gesamtausgabe*, vol. 68, Frankfurt/M: Klostermann 1993.

Dieter Henrich
'Was ist Metaphysik, was Moderne?', in *Merkur*, no. 6, 1986.

Axel Honneth
I 'Integrity and Disrespect: Principles of a Conception of Morality Based on a Theory of Recognition', in A.H., *The Fragmented World of the Social: Essays in Social and Political Philosophy*. Albany: State University of New York Press 1995.
II *The Struggle for Recognition: The Moral Grammar of Social Conflicts*, tr. J. Anderson, Cambridge/Mass.: MIT 1996.

Gary Indiana
Resentment, London: Quartet Books 1998.

Søren Kierkegaard
I *Repetition: An Essay in Experimental Psychology*, tr. Walter Lowrie, Princeton/NJ: Princeton U.P. 1946.
II *Either/Or*, Part II, tr. H.V. and E.H. Hong, Princeton/NJ: Princeton U.P. 1987.

Alexandre Kojève
Introduction à la lecture de Hegel, Paris: Gallimard 1947.

Jacques Lacan
The Ethics of Psychoanalysis, 1957–1960, tr. D. Porter, New York: Norton 1992.

Karl Marx
The Eighteenth Brumaire of Louis Bonaparte, New York: International Publishers 1975.

Christoph Menke
I   'Warum und Wie?', in *Babylon*, nos. 13–14, Frankfurt/M. 1994.
II   *The Sovereignty of Art: Aesthetic Negativity in Adorno and Derrida*, tr. N. Solomon, Cambridge/Mass.: MIT 1998.
III '"Anerkennung im Kampfe". Zu Hegels Jenaer Theorie der Ausdifferenzierung moderner Gesellschaften', in *Archiv für Rechts- und Sozialphilosophie*, vol. 77, 1991.
IV   *Tragödie im Sittlichen. Gerechtigkeit und Freiheit nach Hegel*, Frankfurt/M.: Suhrkamp 1996.
V   'Selbstreflexion der Moral', manuscript 1998.

Luc Montagnier
Des virus et des hommes, Paris: Odile Jacob 1994.

Jean-Luc Nancy
'Lob der Vermischung', in *Lettre international*, no. 5, Berlin 1993.

Friedrich Nietzsche
I   *Beyond Good and Evil*, tr. H. Zimmern, London: Allen & Unwin 1967.
II   *Thus Spoke Zarathustra*, tr. R.J. Hollingdale, Harmondsworth: Penguin 1969.

Hans Erich Nossack
Spirale. Roman einer schlaflosen Nacht, Frankfurt/M.: Suhrkamp 1972.

Grace Paley
Enormous Changes at the Last Minute: Stories, New York: Farrar, Straus and Giroux 1974.

Oriol Pi de Cabanyes
Repensar Catalunya, Barcelona: Edicions 62 1989.

BIBLIOGRAPHY

John Rawls
A Theory of Justice, Cambridge/Mass.: Harvard U.P. 1971.

Hugo Santiago (with Jorge Luis Borges and Adolfo Bioy Casares)
Les autres, Paris: Christian Bourgois 1974.

Nathalie Sarraute
The Use of Speech, tr. B. Wright, London: Calder 1983.

Carl Schmitt
Theorie des Partisanen, Berlin: Duncker und Humboldt 1975.

Gershom Sholem
'Redemption through Sin', tr. H. Halkin, in *The Messianic Idea in Judaism and Other Essays on Jewish Spirituality*, New York: Schocken 1995.

John Searle
'Literary Theory and Its Discontents', in *Beyond Poststructuralism: The Speculations of Theory and the Experience of Reading*, ed. W.V. Harris, University Park: Pennsylvania State U.P. 1996.

Ludwig Siep
Anerkennug als Prinzip der praktischen Philosophie, Freiburg/München: Karl Alber 1979.

Andrew Sullivan
Virtually Normal. An Argument About Homosexuality, London: Picador 1996.

Charles Taylor
'The Politics of Recognition', in C.T. *et al.* (eds), *Multiculturalism and the 'Politics of Recognition'*, Princeton/NJ: Princeton U.P. 1992.

244

Christos Tsiolkas
Loaded, Milsons Point/New South Wales: Viking 1995.

Ernst Tugendhat
Vorlesungen über Ethik, Frankfurt/M.: Suhrkamp 1993.

Paul Valéry
'Note et digression', in P.V., *Oeuvres*, vol. 1, Paris: Gallimard 1957.

Michael Walzer
I   'Two Kinds of Universalism', in Ronald Dworkin *et al.* (eds), *The Tanner Lectures on Human Values XI*, Salt Lake City: University of Utah Press 1990.
II *Spheres of Justice: A Defense of Pluralism and Equality*, New York: Basic Books 1983.

Albrecht Wellmer
The Persistence of Modernity: Essays on Aesthetics, Ethics, and Postmodernism, tr. D. Midgley, Cambridge/Mass.: MIT 1991.

Ludwig Wittgenstein
On Certainty, ed. G.E.M. Anscombe and G.H. Wright, tr. D. Paul and G.E.M. Anscombe, Oxford: Blackwell 1969.

María Zambrano
La agonía de Europa, Madrid: Mondadori 1988.

PHRONESIS

Printed in the United States
by Baker & Taylor Publisher Services